D1007170

# MAE WEST

# MAE WEST

*A Pyramid Illustrated History of the Movies*

by
**MICHAEL BAVAR**

*General Editor:* **TED SENNETT**

**PYRAMID**
**PUBLICATIONS**
**NEW YORK**

**MAE WEST**
**A Pyramid Illustrated History of the Movies**

Copyright © 1975 by Pyramid Communications, Inc.

All rights reserved. No part of this book may be reproduced in any form or by any electronic or mechanical means including information storage and retrieval systems without permission in writing from the Publisher, except by a reviewer who may quote brief passages in a review.

Pyramid edition published October 1975

ISBN 0-515-03868-7

Library of Congress Catalog Card Number 75-18545

Printed in the United States of America

Pyramid Books are published by Pyramid Communications, Inc. Its trademarks, consisting of the word "Pyramid" and the portrayal of a pyramid, are registered in the United States Patent Office.

Pyramid Communications, Inc., 919 Third Avenue, New York, N.Y. 10022

(graphic design by ANTHONY BASILE)

# ACKNOWLEDGMENTS

The author wishes to thank the following for their assistance: Robert Connolly, Aristotle Panagako, Fannie Jeffrey, Giovanna and Patrick Montgomery, and Mike Stephens and Joseph Seechak of Metromedia Television.

*Photographs:* Jerry Vermilye, The Memory Shop,
Kenneth G. Lawrence's Movie Memorabilia Shop,
Gene Andrewski, Cinemabilia, Movie Star News, Quality First,
and the companies that produced the films of Mae West:
Paramount Pictures Corporation, Universal Pictures,
Columbia Pictures and Twentieth Century-Fox Film Corporation

# CONTENTS

From the very beginning, the lady knew who she was and just what she wanted out of life. At age four, Mama and Papa West decided to take little Mae to be photographed. Mae agreed but insisted on posing with a dog that had captured her fancy. The dog had one black ear and one black eye. Papa scoured the neighborhood, bringing home several likely candidates. One by one, Mae rejected the mutts. The situation grew desperate and Papa began to fume. Threats and pleas. All to no avail. There would be no photo session until the little dog with one black ear and one black eye showed up. Papa found the dog . . .

Some twenty years later, a blonde, buxom young lady paid a trip to Chicago's rough-tough South Side. In a raunchy cabaret, the girl watched with delight as the local blacks gyrated to a new beat called the "shimmy shawobble." A few nights later, Mae West was in the middle of her vaudeville turn. In the wings, fellow performers were watching the fun. Looking their way, Mae suddenly went into the shimmy. The theater began to buzz. There were whistles and applause from the balcony, and shouts of joy from the wings. Mae was the girl of the hour . . .

A few years later, a certain Mr. Florenz Ziegfeld knocked on the dressing room door of a young lady

# INTRODUCTION: THE GOSPEL ACCORDING TO MAE WEST

who had been making a big noise on the vaudeville circuit. The great man wanted Miss West to join the cast of his *Follies*. Mae refused—politely but very firmly. The impresario was understandably perplexed. Mae's reasons: Ziegfeld's theaters were too big for the kind of intimate audience contact that her act required. If Ziegfeld could find another theater, well then, maybe . . .

Mae never did work for Ziegfeld but she did go on to write and star in her own Broadway shows. And to do it all with the same independence and self-assurance that must have awed Ziegfeld. When Actors Equity wouldn't let her fire a recalcitrant leading man (one thing Mae never could tolerate), Mae simply closed the show .

A couple of decades later, a very hip lady in her sixties wrote a letter to a man she dubbed the "Mahatma of the Libido." Millions of curious Americans knew him as the High Priest of Sex, Dr. Alfred C. Kinsey. In her epistle, Mae commended the good doctor on his research but gently reminded him that she had come up with most of

11

the same findings several decades earlier. And *her* knowledge didn't come from any test tube. First-hand experience had taught Mae that "sex is a kind of standard equipment of the human species—without which man might just as well be a mollusk or an amoeba." And all this scientific jargon shouldn't make us forget that sex is basically fun. She signed the letter, "Sexsationally yours, Mae West."

Her theme song could well be "My Way." She never for a moment doubted her charisma as a performer. On that subject she has written: "Personality is the glitter that sends your little gleam across the footlights and the orchestra pit into that big black space where the audience is." And Mae had personality to spare.

Her screen image is immediately recognizable: the marcelled wig, the insinuating sneer, the hourglass figure, the hand on full hip, the sashaying walk. Taken as a whole, they form the unique creature known as Mae West. Her screen personality never varies from film to film. She is always tough but good-natured; resilient but determined; bold but self-mocking. The juxtaposition of these highly diverse elements would suggest a complex lady—an Ibsen heroine or a Tennessee Williams neurotic. But no—Mae is as healthy and direct as the honky-tonk music that so often accompanies her entrance.

As a performer, she has always seized the moment. When the scandal of her plays *Sex* and *The Drag* had cooled down, Mae was off to Hollywood to burn up the silver screen. When the public seemed to tire of her movies, Mae abandoned Hollywood for the London stage and the night clubs of Las Vegas. When muscle men went out and rock 'n' roll came in, Mae was right in there pitching. "Baby, Light My Fire" she purred; "There's Gonna Be a Whole Lotta Shakin' Goin' On," she warned. And you had better believe it. When a whole new generation was about to ask —"Who is Mae West?" she returned to the screen in *Myra Breckenridge*. The critics weren't exactly ecstatic. But ten thousand screaming fans—mostly teeny-boppers—lined Broadway to proclaim Mae "Queen of the World," a fact the lady herself had never doubted. Not for one moment.

After a highly successful career as a headliner on Broadway, the notorious author and star of such vehicles as *Sex* and *The Drag* was lured out to Hollywood. For a performer of Mae West's all-consuming ego and magnetic personality, the move was inevitable. She was almost forty—a rather late age for a sex symbol to be burning up the silver screen. Other notable stage artists—Alla Nazimova and Laurette Taylor prominently among them—had made their screen debuts well into their forties. These ladies, however, were trading in other commodities than Mae's.

It was George Raft who provided the impetus for Mae's Western venture. Mae had known Raft since his early days as a professional tango dancer and "gopher" for several of New York's biggest mobsters. *Night after Night* (1932) was Paramount's attempt to mold Raft into the image of Rudolph Valentino. From the hair slicked down with a pint jar of vaseline to the most elegant thirties tailoring, every effort was made to capture Raft's extraordinary resemblance to the famed Latin lover.

Raft plays Joe Anton, a sleek, somewhat ingenuous owner of a fancy clipjoint. The producers wanted a snappy, fast-talking dame as a comic foil for Raft. Texas Guinan was their first choice for the role of Maudie Triplett. Raft

# ENTER MAUDIE TRIPLETT

strongly recommended Mae, whom he thought would be "sensational." The rest, as Mae says, is "history."

*Night after Night* offers a satirical glimpse at a peculiarly American phenomenon: Prohibition. Joe Anton's club is one of Gotham's most elegant watering places. Fancy chandeliers, thick carpets, a jazz orchestra—the ambiance is geared to attract the cream of Broadway's low-lifers and high-lifers. Tough on the outside, Joe is, in reality, a tired, restless, rather sweet guy: "I'm tired of bein' a pal to a lot of drunks." Joe wants more out of life: class, education, and polish. The tale of a low-lifer who wants to pull himself up by the bootstraps is always ripe with comic possibilities. So ripe in fact that it didn't take long for Mae to take a turn at it herself. In 1935, she played her own variation on this theme as cowgirl turned society dame in *Goin' to Town*.

Anton's eye is on one of the club's most alluring attractions, a nightly visitor named Jerry Healy (Constance Cummings). Jerry is the prototype of the twenties "modern woman," a role often associated with Joan Crawford. Wealthy, independent, secure in her

Mae as a "French vamp" in vaudeville

magnificently appointed Park Avenue apartment, Jerry represents a "class act" to Joe. On the surface, Jerry is untouchable, cool, and elegant. Underneath, she smolders, as Joe is soon to discover. When gun moll Iris Dawn (Wynne Gibson) threatens the pair, jealously lashing out at the mobster and "Miss Park Avenue," Jerry cowers. Moments later, out of danger, she overwhelms Joe with her kisses. When Joe storms into Jerry's Art Deco pad, she first turns a disdainful glance and a pair of pouting lips to him, then melts into jelly before his anger.

To be worthy of such a creature, Joe decides to educate himself by employing an Emily Post blueblood named Mabel Jellyman. Played to the hilt by Alison Skipworth, Miss Jellyman believes that education consists of broadening the "a" in "rather" and feeding Joe liberal doses of *Time* Magazine's coverage of the Lausanne Conference and the Russian Five Year Plan.

Joe's plan is to invite Jerry Healy to supper, then proceed to impress her with the worldly knowledge that Miss Jellyman (who will be placed strategically beside him) will draw out subtly. The stage is now set for Mae's entrance. And what an entrance it is! Long years as a vaudeville and stage headliner had taught Mae the importance of the entrance. Consider the situation: an elegant clipjoint, the orchestra playing smooth dance tunes of the twenties, sleek mobster on the make, a white carnation in his elegantly tailored tux, cool Park Avenue beauty, fake Emily Post blueblood chaperone. There is a commotion at the door. "Who's dere?," shouts the goon at the entrance. That inimitable voice: "The fairy princess, ya mug." The music changes from Porter to honky tonk and Mae is on the screen.

*Maudie:* Hey, gorilla . . . c'mere. Where's Joe? I wanna see that little rat. No sale, no sale, I'm gonna see him tonight.

Once in the door, Mae is securely on her way to movie stardom. But for her own highly original style and her determination, however, the opportunity might have been missed. The initial working script proved unacceptable to Mae. The part was "unimportant and banal, the dialogue did nothing for me," she wrote in her autobiography, *Goodness Had Nothing to Do with It*. Restless and disheartened, Mae wanted out. The Paramount bosses panicked. There were negotiations and conferences, and finally, a tentative solution: "I entirely rewrote my part and gave myself my best-styled dialogue. What was good for me was good for the picture." The studio bosses and the director, Archie Mayo, were still unconvinced. "How do you know these

Mae at the height of her stage career

Mae making a silent screen test in New York City

NIGHT AFTER NIGHT (1932). With George Raft

lines are going to be funny, Miss West?'' they demanded. The answer was immediate: "I know audiences. I know what they laugh at and what they expect from me." The powers were still dubious. "Broadway audiences, sure. Now you are going to have motion picture audiences." Mae: "People have eyes and ears and they all laugh at the same things if they are funny." With that display of good sense, Mae won round one of the battle.

Watching the film in progress, Mae became upset with the slowness of the actors. Mae's stage technique had been a surefire one:

"Actors around me work faster—they keep the pace while I take liberties in my timing." Her solution to the problem was swift and uncanny: "I'm going to change my tempo and work fast—very fast—the picture needs a lift, a big lift to pick up the speed and wake an audience up—excite them."

Mae's entrance in *Night after Night* lifts the film bolt upright. Sauntering over to the hatcheck girl, she checks her furs. "Goodness, what beautiful diamonds," the girl murmurs. "Goodness had nothing to do with it, dearie," Mae quips in the first of literally dozens of one-liners that were to become part of

*NIGHT AFTER NIGHT (1932). Maudie deals a hand.*

the American jargon. Mae's idea had been to saunter up the thickly carpeted staircase immediately after her line, the camera following her ample, swaying derrière. "It's what you do after a funny line that helps the laugh. You can cut off the laugh instantaneously ... I don't wait for the laughs. I just sort of roll with the punches." Mae's "punch" didn't suit Archie Mayo and there was another studio crisis. No camera pan, he ordered. "Do it both ways," Mae suggested wisely. The studio bosses "nearly choked" on their cigars during her walk up the stairs. Unfortunately, existing prints of *Night after Night* don't include the controversial scene.

Once securely inside Anton's fashionable clipjoint, Maudie wreaks havoc. Rightly feeling that she will ruin his chances of winning Miss Park Avenue, Joe orders Maudie sent away. But there is no stopping Mae. Coached to rise when a lady enters, Joe springs reluctantly to attention as Maudie descends on the table:

*Maudie:* Joey ... Joey ... c'mere and kiss me, you dog. You're lookin' great. Who's your tailor now? (She gives Jerry the once-over.) Who's the dame?

Introduced to a rather glacially polite Jerry, Maudie quips: "You're not bad, either." Then, to Joe: "Good pickin', honey." The introductions continue:

*Jellyman:* What's your name?

*Maudie:* Maudie Triplett, one of the bluebloods from Kentucky and if you don't like the color, we'll change it.

By now, Joe is getting very hot around his tight, white collar.

*Jellyman (all smiles and good breeding):* Have you had your dinner?

*Maudie:* Yeah, and a lovely one. But I could go for some of that stuff in the bottle.

Clearly uneasy, Joe excuses himself to show Jerry around the place. "Anything you do is O.K. with me," Maudie leers suggestively as the couple departs.

Maudie's camaraderie with Mabel Jellyman is immediate. The ensuing scenes between West and Skipworth, both seasoned veterans of the stage, are surely the highlight of the film. "Do you believe in love at first sight?," coos Jellyman, sighing after the departing Anton and Jerry. "I don't know but it saves an awful lot of time," quips Maudie.

Maudie's job is to break down Jellyman's inhibitions—a task that Mae was to boldly assume in so many of her screen incarnations.

*NIGHT AFTER NIGHT (1932). With George Raft*

*Maudie (filling the glasses):* If you're gonna be Broadway, you gotta learn to take it and you might as well break in the act right now.

*Jellyman:* Maudie, do you really think I could get rid of my inhibitions?

*Maudie:* Why, sure. I got an old trunk you can put 'em in . . . hotcha!

Mae is now the teacher and her poor student ends up with a monumental morning-after hangover. Maudie is bright and alert—no one can drink *her* under the table. She is all smiles and encouragement.

*Maudie: (pouring a drink):* Stick this under your belt. Never mind what it is . . . it'll put you right back on your feet.

*Jellyman:* Chemistry's a wonderful thing.

*Maudie:* I'll say it is. I know a couple of druggists that never made a dime till Prohibition.

Now is the time to break down all of Jellyman's inhibitions. And Maudie has a plan:

*Maudie:* Dearie, you're wastin' time. Why, a gal with your poise and class . . . you'd make thousands in my business.

*Jellyman:* Your business? Are you asking me to come into your business?

*Maudie:* One of the best rackets in the world.

(Jellyman's understandable "misunderstanding" is the stuff from which so many great comic scenes are made.)

*Jellyman:* Of course, you women have been a factor in the building of civilization, protecting our good women, thereby preserving the sanctity of the home . . . (*mumbling*) DuBarry, Cleopatra . . .

Mae fixes her with the soon to be famous (and much imitated) West double-take: "Say, what kinda business ya think I'm in??"

Maudie, it turns out, runs an independent chain of beauty parlors. She's about to open the latest—called "The Institute de Beaut." Maudie makes an offer that poor Mabel can't refuse: "A hundred dollars a week and I'll cut you in on the profits."

With Mabel Jellyman's future a sure success, Maudie has only Joe's romance to manipulate. Sashaying down a corridor, Mabel at her side, she spots Joe and Jerry just ahead. One glance tells her all. "C'mon, Mabel, get out those books," she winks at the lovers. "Looks like

23

1400 - 71

*NIGHT AFTER NIGHT* (1932). With Alison Skipworth and George Raft

he's gonna take more lessons." Fade-out.

Maudie Triplett is the first of Mae's screen creations and, as such, sets the pattern. Maudie is tough, full of snappy talk. She is independent—both in love and business. There are no closed doors for such a woman. She seizes every opportunity: Mabel Jellyman *would* make a classy Institute de Beaut hostess and Maudie is not going to lose her. She's on equal terms with the guys, whether it calls for slapping Joey on the back or giving orders to his butler.

Mae is a "pal" in *Night after Night*, good-naturedly giving advice to men and women alike. This cozy aspect of her screen personality would harden in succeeding films, especially where men are concerned. Mae is soon to become Queen Bee—tough, resilient, bossing men around rather than counseling them.

With the sensational reviews and box-office returns that greeted *Night after Night*, a starring vehicle for Mae West was inevitable. With her unerring instinct and all-consuming ego drive, Mae knew exactly what that vehicle should be—her 1928 stage success, *Diamond Lil*. "I'm her and she's me and we're each other," Mae has said of her unique creation: a powerful, alluring, diamond-hungry music-hall entertainer. Here was the perfect image to establish the West "persona" once and for all time on the screen. And that is exactly what happened. "More people saw me than saw Napoleon, Lincoln and Cleopatra. I was better known than Einstein and Picasso," she wrote in a typical burst of Westian candor. Mae saw her vehicle as more than just an ego-massage, however: "I changed the fashion of two continents. The style of the Gay Nineties became the rage." According to Mae, the Diamond Lil character became a beacon, a symbol of liberation to women everywhere: "Women were trying to walk and talk like me. Women became more sex-conscious—sex was out in the open and fun."

*She Done Him Wrong* (1933) —Paramount felt this title would sell more tickets than *Diamond Lil*—is one of Mae's most lavish films. With her theatrical background, Mae knew the impor-

# LADY LOU

tance of surrounding herself with the finest supporting players and the most beautiful costumes and settings. *She Done Him Wrong* is the Bowery of the nineties brought to vivid life. During the titles, we are treated to a kaleidoscopic view of this fabled area: fancy women mingle with immigrant peddlers, a trained monkey entertains the passengers on a trolley and the barroom boys skim the foam of their beer mugs. This is a tough, dog-eat-dog world, filled with white slavers, corrupt Jewish landlords, and ex-cons. Reigning over all is Lady Lou (Mae West) and she rules with an iron fist in a silk glove.

Mae's entrance is appropriately theatrical. The rowdies in Gus Jordan's saloon are guzzling their pint beer and extolling the "virtues" of Lady Lou. Moments later, the camera pans to a carriage being pulled through the streets. Here is Lady Lou—Floradora hat, parasol, diamonds hanging off her neck, her ears, her wrists, and every finger.

For a film of only sixty-six minutes, the plot is complex, filled with strong encounters, suspense, and an occasional lurid touch. The saloon of Gus Jordan (Noah Beery, Sr.) is a front for his white slaving activities. Gus' accomplices are a fire-breathing moll named Russian Rita (played in high style by

*SHE DONE HIM WRONG (1933). As Lady Lou*

Rafaela Ottiano) and her Russian gigolo, a slick number called Serge Stanieff (Gilbert Roland). The intrigues begin when a lovelorn waif named Sally (Rochelle Hudson) tries to hang herself in the back room of the saloon. Sally is saved in the nick of time, only to be prepared for a worse fate. Gus pawns her off on Rita and Serge who ship poor Sally to a white slaver on the Barbary Coast.

Presiding over the action from her lavish second floor apartment is Lady Lou. Peeking through Lou's keyhole, it is not uncommon to overhear the following:

*Lou:* "You love me so much you'd even frame to get me?"

*Man:* "To get you, I'd even frame my own mother."

Next door to the saloon is the local Salvation Army. Corruption and goodness, side by side. Presiding over this bastion of clean living is Captain Cummings (Cary Grant).

The stage origins of *She Done Him Wrong* are clearly apparent in the work's structure. Basically, the film is a series of short encounters between Lady Lou and the men (and an occasional unwanted female) who take Lou at her word: "Come up sometime 'n' see me."

Lou much prefers a man to accept her open invitation. Nonetheless, when poor Sally is brought in to recuperate from the suicide try, Lou is quick to offer some worldy-wise words of encouragement.

*Lou:* It's always a man.

*Sally:* How'd you know?

*Lou:* It always is . . . takes two to get one in trouble. Men's all alike, married or single. It's their game. I happen to be smart enough to play it their way.

This highly practical bit of advice could easily serve as Lou's motto. For a diamond-hungry dame like Lou, this is the only way to survive. The Bowery is a tough man's world. To be queen, one plays it their way—yet comes out on top.

Lou fixes Sally up with new clothes and sends her on her way: "Always remember to smile. You never have anything to worry about. Forget about this guy. See ya get a good one next time." No West scene is complete without the famous punchline and here Mae supplies one of her most pungent: "When women go wrong, men go right after them." This type of "girl talk" is to become a staple in the West repertoire. Mae loves to pass on her hard-earned knowledge of love and life (is there a difference?) to a willing ear.

Lou's favorite visitor is Captain

*RONG (1933). Lou on the town*

Cummings, the erstwhile director of the mission next door. As is so often the case, the real object of Mae's affections is at first somewhat cold and obdurate—qualities Grant possesses to perfection. The first encounter between Lou and Cummings is terse but pointed:

*Lou:* I always did like a man in a uniform and that one fits you grand. Why don't you come up sometime 'n' see me? I'm home every evening.

*Cummings:* I'm busy every evening.

*Lou:* What are you tryin' to do, insult me?

*Cummings:* I met your kind before.

*Lou:* Come up ... I'll tell your fortune ... (*As he departs*) You can be had ...

This is just the type of challenge that fires Lou. Thus it is not long before she finds the opportunity to exert her legendary powers over Cummings. Their next encounter is rightly the highlight of the film. Cummings comes in search of in-

SHE DONE HIM WRONG (1933). With Gilbert Roland and Rafaela Ottiano

*SHE DONE HIM WRONG* (1933). With Cary Grant

formation about Sally and finds himself the target of Lady Lou's step-by-step plan for seduction:

*Cummings (admiring her jewelry):* So this is your famous collection?

*Lou:* This is just my summer jewelry. Ya oughta see my winter stuff. Ya know it was a toss-up whether I go in for diamonds or sing in the choir. The choir lost.

*Cummings (glibly):* Wonderful . . . but they always seem too cold to me. They have no warmth . . . no soul. I'm sorry you think more of your diamonds than you do of your soul.

*Lou (inevitably):* I'm sorry you think more of my soul than you do of my diamonds. Maybe I ain't got no soul.

*Cummings (a bit lofty):* Oh, yes, you have but you keep it hidden under a mask. You'll wake up and find it sometime. Haven't you ever met a man who could make you happy?

*Lou:* Sure, lots of times.

Though the net is out, Lou is not the kind to sit around waiting. A plan is immediately formulated. Lou will buy the building that houses Cummings' mission. Into her lair she summons Jacobson (Lee Kohlmar), land boss of the Bowery. Jacobson is another in the unfortunate parade of Jewish caricatures that move unashamedly through the Hollywood films of the thirties.

*Jacobson (fingers working feverishly, accent exaggerated Mittel Europa):* You want me to buy some of your famous diamonds?

When Lou tells him what she's really after, Jacobson's manner becomes shifty: "You mean how much if I'm selling or how much if I'm paying taxes?"

*Lou:* Now, stop multiplyin'. I don't wanna buy the Bowery.

*Jacobson:* $25,000!

*(Silence and a stony gaze from hard-driving Lou.)*

*Jacobson:* My own brother couldn't buy for $20,000.

*(Silence . . . more shuffling about.)*

*Jacobson:* For you I'll make it $15,000.

*(No deal. Jacobson starts for the door. This always works. That is, it always did until he started dealing with Lady Lou.)*

In a triumph of double-dealing Lou holds out for $12,000 and even gets the place without a mortgage.

*SHE DONE HIM WRONG* (1933). With Cary Grant

SHE DONE HIM WRONG (1933). With Dewey Robinson
and Owen Moore

The deal is consummated with a magnificent diamond necklace. "Handle it with care," Lou drawls ruefully. "They're only my heart." How right she is. Jacobson wonders if the diamonds are paste. Lou: "You never heard of me cheatin' anyone, did ya?" Jacobson: "No, not about money."

It is hardly just coincidence that Lou's next visitor comes bearing diamonds. It is the gigolo Serge offering Rita's diamond pin in return for an hour of Lou's charms. Although the ensuing scene serves basically to push the plot forward, the West humor is not lacking:

*Serge:* I could not stay away.

*Lou:* I kinda expected that ...

*Serge:* I bring you a gift ... I know you love them so.

*Lou (unabashed and sheer delight):* Ain't it grand?

*Serge:* They make your eyes sparkle and your teeth gleam like pearls. The men of my country go wild about women with yellow hair.

*Lou:* I'm glad you told me. I wanna keep straight on my geography.

SHE DONE HIM WRONG (1933). "Why don't you come up
sometime 'n' see me?"

*Serge:* You were made for love and love only. Surely you have enough diamonds.

*Lou:* Diamonds is my career.

*Serge:* I swear I shall die to make you happy.

*Lou:* You wouldn't be much use to me dead. *(Accent on the word "use".)*

At this torrid moment, Rita enters, outraged, and turns on the lovers. Serge is sent off, there are more heated words and then a hair-pulling bout between the ladies. When Rita flashes a stiletto, a struggle ensues and Rita is accidentally stabbed to death. Hearing men's voices, Lou must think fast. Her solution is ingenious—they always are with West. When the door opens, Rita is propped up in a chair and Lou is nonchalantly combing her long tresses. This delightfully lurid touch of melodrama is totally appropriate to the shady dealings at Gus Jordan's.

Lou is as much in control of the situation outside her lavish digs as she is inside. On a field trip to Joliet to visit her old beau Chick Clark (Owen Moore), Lou saunters through the prison like a queen

*SHE DONE HIM WRONG (1933). Lou and her Captain Cummings*

bestowing knighthoods. The convicts gaze hungrily out of their bars as she sashays past. This image of a double line of eager males watching Mae pass by is to reoccur throughout her career; in future films, in nightclubs, right up to *Myra Breckenridge*. Lou is greeted on all sides. "What is this, ole home week?" she quips delightedly. (Mae likes nothing better than to throw one-liners at a bunch of adoring males.)

Lou's encounters with Chick provide a valuable insight into our heroine. Clark is in the clink because he got caught stealing diamonds for Lou. "You'd sell your heart and lungs for a handful of diamonds," he accuses. Chick talks tough to Lou: "If you been double crossin' me, you gonna pay for it." He gets Lou to promise that she will wait for him. Then he melts into jelly before her beauty and manipulative powers—the inevitable pattern.

When Chick gets out, having jumped freight and "crawled through da mud" to get back to Gus Jordan's, Lou treats him with disdain. "None of them cheap threats. I tell ya you're through." Chick approaches, blood in his eye. Lou stands unmoved, aglitter with her diamonds. Chick falls sobbing at her feet: "Ain't ya got a heart left in ya?" All men are ultimately putty in the hands of such as Lou. The film's conclusion is strange

and thoroughly unconvincing. Captain Cummings, it turns out, is an undercover agent for the police. He breaks up Gus Jordan's gang, then puts the handcuffs on Lou:

*Lou:* Those absolutely necessary? You know, I wasn't born with them!

*Cummings:* All those men would have been a lot safer if you had.

*Lou:* I don't know . . . hands ain't everything.

The situation looks desperate for Lou. For the first time, she seems to have been outwitted. "My wrap," she purrs. Will her powers of seduction triumph? Inside the paddy wagon, Cummings unexpectedly slips a gold band on her finger: Lou looks up at him as if she expected it all along:

*Lou (purring):* Dark and handsome . . .

*Cummings:* You bad girl . . .

*Lou:* You'll find out . . .

*(Fade-out)*

Unrealistic and unconvincing it may be, but it offers further proof that there is no situation that Mae West can't maneuver. Even the arms of the law can be used for an embrace.

Mae's next screen incarnation was Tira, the circus queen of *I'm No Angel* (1933). Tira is one of Mae's most exotic creations—a modern day Circe who tames man and beast alike. She is the link between two different worlds: the honky-tonk carnival existence with its cheap thrills and the posh Park Avenue milieu with its smart clubs and perfumed women. That Tira moves freely and securely in both worlds proves that she is undisputed empress of all domains.

At the carnival, Tira tames lions and breaks hearts. On Park Avenue, Tira is a white princess surrounded by black slaves. Tira's entrance provides Mae with another of her spectacular attention-getters. A raucous carney barker spews out every superlative in his vocabulary: "Miss Tira, the vision of supreme pulchritude . . . the only show in town where the tickets are made of asbestos." A huge crowd of men surges forward hungrily. A red carpet is ceremoniously rolled out. Spotlights. Trumpets. And now Tira herself, bumping and grinding to the delight of the men who gawk and drool in ecstasy.

Tira is a highly independent creature. When Big Bill Barton (Edward Arnold) reproaches Tira for spending her nights off the grounds, she counters:

*Tira:* I ain't the same as the rest of yas . . . I'm sick of people

# THE FABULOUS TIRA

worryin' about what I do . . .

*Big Bill:* Gettin' high hat? *(Approaches menacingly.)* Take that as a warning.

*Tira (in the best sassy West manner):* You take it . . . and bury it. Maybe it'll grow lilies.

Like Lady Lou, Tira has an eye for the jewels. During her shimmy, she notes a huge rock on the pinky of one of the locals. A wink and a leer, and a date is fixed. The ensuing scene with her new beau, Ernest Brown (William B. Davidson) is full of West quips. Tira's habit is to lure men to her hotel room, make love to them, then rob them. Brown is her present victim.

*Tira:* Are ya married or single?

*Brown:* Married five times . . .

*Tira:* Marriage bells must sound like an alarm clock to you.

*Brown:* I don't suppose you believe in marriage, do you?

*Tira:* Only as a last resort . . . *(Beginning to vamp him, cigarette poised.)* Ah . . . what d'ya do for a livin'?

*Brown:* Sort of a politician . . .

*Tira:* I don't like work, either . . .

*I'M NO ANGEL (1933). As Tira*

Tira's taste for males and petty thievery is tempered by an interest in the occult. (West, herself, devotes many chapters in her autobiography to this fascinating subject.) "My whole life is ruled by astrology," Tira exclaims. "I wouldn't make a move without it." Tira's guru is a carnival phony called the Rajah (Nigel de Brulier). His presence lends a hint of occult powers to our honky-tonk Circe and also provides West with some delightful one-liners:

*Rajah:* I see a change.

*Tira:* What? A change of men?

*Rajah:* A change of position . . .

*Tira:* Sitting or reclining?

Tira's faith in the Rajah is naïve and rather refreshing: "Somewhere there's a guy with a million waitin' for a dame like me. Rajah said so."

Mae's most spectacular scene in *I'm No Angel* is the celebrated lion taming act. In her autobiography, Mae insists that she told Paramount: "The lion scene is the main reason I'm doing the picture." Since childhood, Mae relates, she had been obsessed with a "driving, fiery compulsion" to tame a lion.

*I'M NO ANGEL (1933). With Nigel de Brulier*

*I'M NO ANGEL (1933). Tira tames a lion.*

*I'M NO ANGEL (1933).*
*Tira on the midway*

*I'M NO ANGEL (1933). With her ladies-in-waiting*

She would often visit the zoo just to be able to stand before the lions' cage, "to visualize myself in full command inside the bars."

With the eye of a born story-teller, West sets the scene for her daring feat. The head trainer at Paramount, we are told, had his arm almost torn off preparing the animals for the scene. Consequently the studio ordered men stationed at vantage points outside the cage, their rifles loaded with live ammunition. Mae enters the cage: "I began to move, cracking my whip. I could feel the lions surrendering to my will as they stared at me with their great, beautiful, fas-

cinating, dangerous eyes, fascinating me. They, too, seemed to be fascinated by this stranger in dazzling gold and white."

Mae describes her emotions in highly-charged terms: " . . . excitement began to take ahold of me, multiplied a thousand-fold, charging me with electric voltage, until I could see nothing, hear nothing, feel nothing but an overpowering sense of increasing mastery that mounted, higher and higher until it gratified every atom of the obsession that had driven me." Circe indeed!

On screen, the lion taming act *almost* lives up to Mae's own excitement about filming it. The barker loudly informs the huge crowd that what they are about to witness is unparalleled since Nero threw the Christians to the lions. "You will see feminine beauty—triumphant and unafraid—defy death by placing her head in the jaws of the King of the Beasts." Tira is preceded by six strapping athletes who sound their trumpets. The curtains part and she appears, resplendent in white and gold atop an elephant. Tira is then led around the ring to the wild adulation of the crowd.

Once inside the ring, Tira shoots off her pistol, cracks the whip and, in general, handles the beasts like she handles her men. "C'mon," she snarls to a particularly sluggish specimen, "get up there . . . you'll end up as a rug, ya mug!" When her four-footed friend yawns, Mae drawls: "Where were you last night?" Coaxing another beast into action, she purrs: "Come on, handsome, say ah" and in goes her head. The crowd is beside itself.

Among the "swells" in the grandstand is Kirk Lawrence (Kent Taylor), a socialite who acts as the catalyst for Tira's move from carnival world to Park Avenue splendor. Backstage after her triumph, Tira entertains Kirk, his jealous fiancée Alicia (Gertrude Michael), and their party:

*Tira:* I had to shoot a lion once . . .

*Society Lady:* Really? Was he mad?

*Tira:* Well he wasn't exactly pleased about it . . .

The party loves Tira's vulgar, hip-swinging sassiness and she basks in their delight. In this heady atmosphere, Kirk loses his head (naturally) and falls under Tira's spell. He plants his walking stick in her potted plant, then leaves murmuring:

*Kirk:* You've been awfully kind . . . I'll never forget you.

*Tira:* No one ever does . . .

Moments later, he is back in search of his hidden stick. The love scene that follows is a masterpiece of subtle suggestiveness—the kind of scene only Mae West could bring off.

*Kirk:* I know right where I left it.

*Tira:* You got a good memory.

*Kirk:* I ought to, since I left it here on purpose.

*Tira (with an admiring glance):* You planted that stick?

*Kirk:* Sure . . . I had to find a way to see you alone. You're dazzling, you're beautiful, you're gorgeous . . .

47

*I'M NO ANGEL (1933). Tira in her "spider" dress*

*Tira:* Wait a minute . . . wait a minute . . . . take it slower . . .

By some magic formula manufactured in the Hollywood of the thirties, we next find Tira ensconced in a Park Avenue apartment. A bevy of black maids surround their white princess. Mae tended to favor blacks as confidantes and sidekicks. She was justly proud of being among the first stars to further the cause of the black screen performer. Louise Beavers had done the honors in *She Done Him Wrong*. In *I'm No Angel*, Mae is surrounded by Libby Taylor and Gertrude Howard, among others. Tira jokes with her maids, sings to them about the game of romance, and even does a shuffle number to their unabashed delight. They, in turn, dress her, comb her hair, buff her nails and, in general, fuss over their mistress. This does not prevent them from spying on her lovers with much giggling and rolling of the eyes.

Into this lair comes Kirk's cousin, Jack Clayton (Cary Grant). Like Captain Cummings of *She Done Him Wrong*, Clayton is a man with a mission. He has come to persuade Tira to give up the lovesick Kirk. Mae receives Grant garbed in a negligee covered with spider webs. A huge spider scarab completes the motif. In his cold, suave manner, Clayton comes up with all the usual arguments: "Kirk's been neglecting his business, his fiancée Alicia, etc. etc." Tira has been giving Clayton the once over during his little prepared speech and from the look on Mae's face, we know that she's already thrown Kirk over for his handsome emissary.

*Clayton:* Do you mind if I get personal?

*Tira:* Go right ahead. I don't mind if you get familiar . . .

Maneuvering Clayton onto a sofa, she melts his hauteur and gives him a framed photo of herself as circus queen.

*Clayton:* You've been wonderful . . .

*Tira (purring):* You been kinda wonderful yourself.

All business again, Clayton reminds her of his mission, but Tira has other things on her mind.

*Tira:* I can't promise anything right now but ya started a new trend of thought in my mind.

Tira's other scene with Clayton exists mainly to give Mae a chance to use Grant as a sounding board for some snappy one-liners. The results are pure gold:

*I'M NO ANGEL (1933). With Cary Grant*

*Clayton:* You were wonderful tonight.

*Tira:* I'm always wonderful at night.

*Clayton (feeding it to her):* Tonight I thought you were especially good.

*Tira:* When I'm good I'm very good. But when I'm bad I'm better.

*Clayton:* If I could only trust you . . .

*Tira:* You can . . . *(West pause.)* Hundreds have.

The climax of *I'm No Angel* is an extended trial sequence which is as much a vehicle for Queen Mae as her lion taming act. Tira brings Clayton to court for breach of promise. Her outfit is smashing: a simple floor-length black gown, long strand of pearls (the touch of simplicity that gives class), a fur wrap and a chapeau of feathers drawn tightly over her marcelled wig. Mae acts as defense lawyer, prosecutor, and inevitably the judge at this case. She sasses Clayton's lawyer:

*Lawyer:* You've been on friendly terms with several men . . .

*I'M NO ANGEL (1933). Tira argues her case.
On the stand: Ralf Harolde*

*Tira:* All right, I was the sweetheart of Sigma Psi, so what?

One by one, Tira's old boyfriends are led into the cage, only to have Mae crack the whip and send them off groveling. Everyone is present for the act, including maid Beulah who howls with delight everytime her mistress scores a point. Mae vamps the jury, twists the judge around her bejeweled finger, and, in general, outclasses every competitor.

Tira first demolishes old beau Ernest Brown: "Ain't you the man with five wives . . . and you was married to one of 'em when you stepped out with me, wasn't ya?" Tira won't let Brown get a word in and finally silences his splutterings with a well-aimed "cheat!" The jury roars, as Mae dismisses him curtly: "O.K. I'm through with you." Next on the docket is Kirk Lawrence, polished and urbane as ever:

*Tira:* You're not lookin' to get those presents back. You gave me those nuggets cause you liked me a little, didn't you? I didn't ask you for them.

*Kirk:* I don't regret giving them to you.

*Tira:* You were engaged to marry a girl when you came up.

*Kirk:* I broke it off . . .

*Tira:* So whaddya cryin' about?

Tira hits each man exactly where he lives—and in doing so, exposes their supercilious double standard of behavior where women are concerned.

She is relentless in her cross-examinations. Clayton's eager beaver lawyer tries to object but by now the judge is a slave to Tira's vampish charms. He overrides every objection. "You're right, judge," Mae quips.

After the trial, there is the inevitable press conference with Tira again the center of adulation and attention. Flashbulbs pop as eagerly as the questions. A doting female reporter asks, "Why do you admit having so many men in your life?," and Mae replies with one of her classic lines: "It's not the men in your life, it's the life in your men that counts."

The following scene is one of Mae's most inspired. Tira is at the door of her luxurious apartment, bidding the judge goodbye: "Come up and see me anytime," she drawls. He slobbers and exits. The phone rings. As Mae crosses to answer, we see that the room is bulging with floral tributes. Tira picks up the phone and learns that it's one of the jurors. Presumably they've all been phoning and sending flowers. "Come up 'n' see me, sometime," Tira purrs.

Clayton arrives, and differences are settled in flash:

*Clayton:* I'm crazy about you.

*Tira:* I did my best to make you that way.

*Clayton:* What are you thinking about?

*Tira (giving Grant a look the censors couldn't do a thing about):* Same thing you are . . .

Mae sings "I'm No Angel," and the film draws to its joyous conclusion.

After *I'm No Angel*, the censors bore down harder than ever on Mae. During the filming of *Belle of the Nineties* (1934), Mae found the Hays official on the set every day—"enjoying himself." For a comedienne of such unique and specialized gifts, this intrusion must have been a constant source of frustration and unhappiness. "I resented the type of censorship that quibbled over every line as if the devil were hiding behind each word," Mae writes.

The censor's cruelest cuts came during the film's opening scenes. Ruby Carter (Mae) takes her boxer boyfriend Tiger Kid (Roger Pryor) up to her apartment. Tiger is in training. Nonetheless he can't resist Ruby. Mae's idea was to get laughs by implying that Tiger not only spent the night but actually went for Mae's specialized kind of "training" for a period of several days. Her idea was to use what she terms "dissolves" to show the passage of time. Unfortunately, she reports, "the censor didn't laugh and he cut."

Censorship problems aside, *Belle of the Nineties* still emerges as a mildly entertaining West vehicle. The plot—the usual underworld melodrama—exists mainly to provide Mae with a series of elaborate production numbers. Director Leo McCarey succeeds brilliantly in capturing Mae's ambiance, from the St. Louis music hall with its buxom chorines and slick-haired crooners to the plush nightspots and sweaty gyms of New Orleans.

No longer just the queen of the circus or the belle of the Bowery, Mae is now Ruby Carter, "the most talked about woman in America," a music hall entertainer and courtesan supreme. The film's structure is a simple one: the conquering woman from St. Louis sets out to win new territories. The characters are the stock ones from the West repertoire: assorted boyfriends, lovers, Mae, and a jealous girlfriend.

Mae's opening number in *Belle* is the most spectacular in all her films. Garbed in designer Travis Banton's most exotic confections, she appears in a variety of fantastic guises: a gigantic rose, a spider, a bat and a butterfly (with fanciful wings like a Japanese kite). The climax of this extravaganza is Mae's incarnation as the Statue of Liberty. Torch held proudly aloft and wrapped in red, white, and blue, Mae brings the shouting music hall audience to its feet. When *Belle* was released, *Vanity Fair* featured Mae as Bartholdi's famed colossus and critic George Jean Nathan dubbed her "the Statue of Libido."

As Ruby Carter, Mae is her

## MISS RUBY CARTER

BELLE OF THE NINETIES (1934). As Ruby

usual flirtatious, independent self. When the steamboat docks at New Orleans, Ruby sashays down the gangplank, arm in arm with playboy millionaire Brooks Claybourne (John Mack Brown). The men at portside surge forward eagerly, and one asks, "Are you in town for good?" Mae replies, "I expect to be here but not for good."

In New Orleans, Ruby is set up as the leading attraction at Ace Lamont's fancy gambling club. Ace (John Miljan) is simply a nastier version of Gus Jordan. Instead of trading in white slaves, this mobster fixes fights. Tough and suave on the exterior, Ace is weak-kneed when it comes to the charms of Ruby Carter:

*Ace:* You and I could go a long way together. With your beauty and my business ability, we could make a fortune. You know why I brought you down here, don't you?

*Ruby:* I had a rough idea.

*Ace:* You're the kind of woman I've dreamed about . . . always desired. I'm wild about you.

*Ruby:* Some of the wildest men make the best pets.

BELLE OF THE NINETIES (1934). With Roger Pryor

*BELLE OF THE NINETIES (1934). Another view*

*BELLE OF THE NINETIES (1934). Ruby and her admirers*

*BELLE OF THE NINETIES (1934). The center of attraction*

*Ace:* Ruby, I must have you. Your golden hair, your fascinating eyes, your alluring smile and lovely arms . . .

*Ruby:* Wait a minute, is this a proposal or are ya takin' inventory?

Even this classic put-down cannot deter Ace, and his machinations provide the plot with endless melodramatic turns. Ace hires Tiger—who just coincidentally happens to end up in New Orleans and not in search of Ruby—to fight for him. To get money for the match, Ace arranges for Tiger to steal Ruby's most precious possession, a fabulous diamond necklace given to her by playboy Brooks. Disguised as a road bandit, Tiger waylays Ace and Ruby in their carriage and snatches the gems.

No one steals Mae's diamonds and gets away with it. From *She Done Him Wrong,* we know that diamonds are this girl's best friend. If she's smart enough to get 'em, she's smart enough to get 'em back. Thus, it doesn't take Ruby long to put two and two together. Why, for instance, did that mysterious robber ignore the rock on Ace's pinky? One hint leads to another. Ever on the alert, Ruby eavesdrops on Ace and Tiger one night. The truth is out.

Revenge is swift. The night of Tiger's big bout, Ruby arrives with Ace, garbed in her finest Travis Banton apparel. Round after round passes by—until Ruby settles her score. Like a blond Lucrezia Borgia, Ruby slips a mickey into Tiger's drinking water, then tells Ace to offer a swig to the exhausted fighter. Moments later, Tiger falls flat on his handsome mug. As she sashays out, Ruby smashes the evidence into smithereens with her train. She exits arm in arm with a perplexed and crestfallen Ace.

The revenge motif runs throughout *Belle,* giving the film what little structure it has. Early in the film, Ruby and Tiger find their romantic tryst almost squelched by vigilant trainer Kirby (James Donlan). To show who's boss, Ruby lets Kirby parade back and forth underneath her windows—in the pouring rain. Kirby takes his revenge by tricking Tiger into thinking that Ruby is a two-timer.

In the film there is even a character bent on vengeance in the person of Molly (Katherine DeMille), Ace's moll. Molly fumes and splutters her way through reel after reel, vainly trying to get back at Ruby for stealing Ace away.

Ruby's true friends, those free of jealousy and petty intrigues, are the blacks: maid Jasmine (Libby Taylor) and her cohorts. Libby serves as a foil for Mae's quips: "Don't let a man put anything over on ya 'cept an umbrella." Libby's boyfriend, a coach driver, takes Libby to a revival meeting. As

*BELLE OF THE NINETIES (1934). Ruby settles an old score.*

*BELLE OF THE NINETIES (1934). "The most talked-about woman in America"*

Ruby intones "Troubled Waters" from a nearby balcony, the blacks cavort feverishly, eyes rolling, hands waving in what seems to be a parody of *The Green Pastures*. Ruby's face is even superimposed on the dancers at this bacchanalia.

Things are on sounder artistic ground in the person of Duke Ellington and his band. Ellington provides the accompaniment for Mae's St. Louis music hall numbers with such style and grace that the expense of having him in the picture for such a short time is more than justified. Ellington was the first in a line of top orchestra leaders—Louis Armstrong and Xavier Cugat were to follow—who back Mae up and lend class to the proceedings.

"Mae West goes modern with seven leading men" ... "Mae's a streamlined gal now—it increases her speed and cuts down resistance" ... "Mae will slay you when she sings grand opera," the publicity hawks shouted in advance of West's next Paramount film, *Goin' to Town* (1935). Alexander Hall directed this fast-paced, snappy tale with finesse, shuttling his star from the saloons and corrals of the Wild West to the Southampton of ancestral mansions and opera balls. Travis Banton was again pressed into service, and his costumes set a new standard for lavishness on the screen.

Mae plays Cleo Borden, a dance hall dame whose prevailing philosophy is directly opposite to Annie Oakley's: You *can* get a man with a gun. Before we even meet Cleo, the men at the local saloon clue us in on what to expect: "Five minutes with her and a guy's lucky to get away with his vaccination." Cleo's boyfriend is Buck Gonzales (Fred Kohler, Sr.), a variation on the powerful tough guy who so often appeals to Mae:

*Buck:* You ain't scared of me cause they say I'm a bad man?

*Cleo:* I'm a good woman for a bad man.

Buck's idea is marriage. For Cleo, that's "a new kind of racket."

# QUEEN CLEO

*Buck:* I'm rich. I'll give you my ranch. Everything I own.

*Cleo:* You certainly make it sound attractive.

In typical West fashion, Cleo rolls dice with Buck. She drives a hard bargain: "Get this straight, if I win, I don't marry you ... I get that strip of land on the Delta." Buck: "And if you lose you marry me." Cleo: "Yes and I get everything you got." The best way to treat a tough guy is with iron gloves.

Cleo loses ... but not for long. Buck is killed on a cattle rustling expedition, leaving Cleo the wealthiest woman on the Delta. At the litigation trial, the judge reminds Cleo that she is now a woman with problems:

*Judge:* Let me remind you to look out for crooks.

*Cleo:* Let the crooks look out for themselves.

Buck's manager, Winslow (Gilbert Emery) is retained to handle affairs. "I'll look after the cattle and the men for you," he announces. "Just the cattle," Cleo drawls. "I'll take care of the men."

Cleo has wealth, power, and a magnificent ranch house filled with

*GOIN' TO TOWN (1935). Queen Cleo in her boudoir*

GOIN' TO TOWN (1935). With Ivan Lebedeff

stuffed animals. But for the moment, no man. On an inspection trip of her vast properties, Cleo spots a good-looking surveyor named Carrington (Paul Cavanagh). The chemical reaction is immediate—as is always the case with Mae. Paul Cavanagh followed Cary Grant as the suave British type who first offers resistance, then falls prey to Mae's special charms. Elegant, trim of figure, and with a tiny moustache, Carrington plays the game very coolly. Undaunted, Cleo shoots off his hat, then lassoes him. Carrington will have none of this uncouth brand of femininity and the battle is on:

*Carrington:* What do you mean by shooting at me? I don't happen to be a target ... not even for somebody like you.

*Cleo:* What do you know about me?

*Carrington:* Just what I see and that's quite sufficient.

*Cleo:* You're easily satisfied.

*Carrington:* What do you want of me?

*GOIN' TO TOWN (1935). With Paul Cavanagh*

*GOIN' TO TOWN (1935). With Ivan Lebedeff and Paul Cavanagh*

*Cleo:* Nothing . . . *(pregnant West pause)* . . . yet.

*Carrington:* You possess an extraordinary sense of humor.

*Cleo:* Yes . . . and that ain't all.

Even Winslow is shocked by Cleo's bold courtship and warns her that you can't get a man with a gun. Cleo's reply is instant: "Oh, yeah?"

Her next assault on Carrington is by night—the best time for a West seduction. Cleo summons him to the ranch house to look over some blueprints. The ensuing scene is a veritable lexicon of Mae's comic techniques: innuendos, insinuations, glances, quips, one-liners, the works. Still livid from the afternoon's encounter, Carrington coldly resists the opening barrage of West charm, unfurls his map, and gets down to business. So does Cleo.

*Carrington:* This represents the undeveloped territory.

*Cleo (vamping):* Hmmm . . . we'll have to do something about that. *(Looking over his shoulder.)* Is it possible there's something you've overlooked?

*Carrington:* I can assure you that you are getting the most out of all this property.

*Cleo (purring):* How can you be sure?

Cleo now tries a new tactic, a watered-down version of the afternoon's assault.

*Cleo:* C'mon, why don't you release those brakes?

*Carrington:* I don't know what you mean.

*Cleo:* You're one of those guys with principles . . . kinda different. You been used to dames who drink pink tea and stick out their little fingers when they drink it.

*Carrington (a hint of involvement, maybe even awe):* This is the first time I ever came in contact with a woman like you.

*Cleo:* If I can help it, it won't be the last. I can be different if I want to. You ain't seen my better side yet.

*Carrington:* You're a dangerous woman.

*Cleo:* Thanks . . . you look good to me, too.

Like all the West heroines, Cleo is highly adaptable. If the old tactics don't get you what you want, try new ones. "I'll take a shot at this lady business," she informs Winslow, places her prize horse Cactus in the International Sweepstakes, and heads for Buenos Aires.

It doesn't take long for Cleo to become the darling of the pampas.

GOIN' TO TOWN (1935). With Lucio Villegas

GOIN' TO TOWN (1935). Cleo surrounded by admirers

*GOIN' TO TOWN (1935). With Gilbert Emery, Tom Monk, Tito Coral, and Marjorie Gateson*

At the racetrack, the international playboys line up by the dozens, and in the elegant dining room of the swank hotel, every eye at every table turns to gaze at Mae, resplendent in a Travis Banton creation. Cleo turns to Winslow: "Those guys must be gentlemen. They all got white shirts on."

The sweepstakes is the key scene in the first half of *Goin' to Town*. Director Hall captures all the fierce excitement and glamor of the event. An added plot twist helps to provide suspense. Cleo's brassy ways and blatant display of wealth offend a certain Mrs. Crane Brittany (Marjorie Gateson). Mrs. Brittany is used to running the prize horse and she's not about to let this blonde upstart become queen for the day. Mrs. Brittany's gigolo is a Russian named Ivan (Ivan Lebedoff), who is a slimier version of the Gilbert Roland character in *She Done Him Wrong*. At first Cleo falls for his line. "Cigarette me, Cossack," she drawls as he starts an elegant pitch about his titled ancestors. "Find me a guy with blue

70

blood in his veins and red ink in his bankbook and I'll marry him," Cleo drawls. But she soon realizes that he's an empty fool and treats him accordingly.

*Cleo:* We're intellectual opposites.

*Ivan:* What do you mean?

*Cleo:* I'm intellectual and you're opposite.

*Ivan (bristling):* I'm an aristocrat and the backbone of my family.

*Cleo:* Your family oughta see a chiropractor.

Mrs. Brittany persuades Ivan to injure Cleo's horse but the plan backfires when Cleo's trusted Taho (Tito Coral) catches Ivan in the act.

Who should turn up at this posh watering spot but Carrington. Cleo teases him, flaunts her Russian consorts, then openly confronts him:

*Cleo:* I can get anything money can buy.

*Carrington:* There happen to be a few things beyond the reach of money. Natural good breeding . . . culture, for another.

*Cleo:* I see you'd like to have my

*GOIN' TO TOWN (1935). With Luis Alberni*

*GOIN' TO TOWN* (1935).
*Cleo practices her singing.*

ancestors go over and come back on the Mayflower.

At the victory dinner for Cleo, her trusted Winslow thwarts the suicide attempt of playboy millionaire Fletcher Colton (Monroe Owsley). Colton has lost every cent at the roulette wheel. Winslow proves to be a man after Cleo's own heart by proposing a very special business deal: If Colton will marry Cleo Borden, he will be permanently out of debt. Colton swallows hard, blinks a couple of times, and then is ushered into Queen Cleo's presence. "You made a swell deal," she trills. Then joyously: "I'm gonna be Mrs. Fletcher Colton of New York, Miami and Southampton."

Ensconced in the ancestral Long Island home, Cleo proceeds to junk all the family portraits. She also adds a well-endowed statue of a Greek athlete to the salon. By delightful coincidence, Colton turns out to be the nephew of Cleo's old nemesis, Mrs. Crane Brittany. When Mrs. Brittany hears what's going on in the family mansion, she gathers her legions and prepares the assault. Mae always relished a confrontation scene, especially one in which she could take pot shots at the phony and the hypocritical. Her aim in *Goin' to Town* is deadly.

*Snob:* Speaking of relatives, Mrs. Colton, have your ancestors ever been traced?

*Cleo:* Why, yes, but they were too smart—they couldn't trace 'em.

*Snob:* You're going to find it raather quiet here after the way *you've* been used to living.

*Cleo:* Don't let that worry you. I expect to put life in the old joint.

*Mrs. Brittany:* I could give you some advice if you asked me.

*Cleo:* You don't ask your enemy how to win the war.

*Mrs. Brittany:* I'll drive you out of Southampton!

To consolidate her position in Long Island society, Cleo decides to throw a super-spectacular bash: "Some high-class entertainment that'll put another 0 in the 400's." The highlight of this event? An opera. Cleo's choice? *Samson and Delilah*—"a lady barber who made good." Thus Mae fulfills another of her childhood ambitions to play the fabled temptresses and powerful queens of history and legend. The opera ball is naturally the key scene of *Goin' to Town*'s second half and as such is as full of spectacle, humor, and melodrama as the Argentinian sweepstakes. All Long Island, it seems, turns out to pay homage to Mrs. Fletcher Colton, the centerpiece of this splashy affair.

Cleo's preparations are almost as

much fun as the performance. As the guests wait eagerly—Carrington prominently among them —the orchestra tunes up. Cleo is given a bit of last minute coaching by Professor Vitola (Luis Alberni) who frets and fumes over her high C. The maid tries desperately to hook up the costume. The violins play her cue and Cleo is on.

The curtains part: A bevy of Nubian slaves (no matter that this is ancient Gaza) crouches expectantly. Delilah appears, sporting blonde tresses and brass breastplates. She steps over the slaves, who submit obediently. A snap of the fingers and they back out. Samson appears. "C'mere Sammy," Cleo drawls, then launches into a very respectable rendition of "Mon coeur s'oeuvre à ta voix." Mae warbles in more than passable French but omits the high C. Cleo plays with Sammy's braids and in general, more than fulfills Saint-Saëns' expectations for the role.

The suspense in this sequence is created by nemesis Mrs. Brittany and her Ivan. Now more than ever determined to run Cleo out of Long Island, Mrs. Brittany hires Ivan to seduce Cleo at the party, thereby hoping to expose and disgrace her. Ivan hides in Cleo's boudoir, awaiting her exit after "Mon coeur." Instead of Cleo, however, it is hubby Colton who arrives. The inveterate gambler is in search of ready cash to pay off his mounting debts. He heads straight for Cleo's strongbox, discovers Ivan, and in the ensuing confrontation, he is accidentally killed. All this to the offscreen music of the *Samson* "Bacchanalia."

Cleo arrives in the first flush of her triumph. There are a myriad of plot turns and complications from this point, the upshot being that Ivan is thwarted, Cleo gets Carrington, and the whole delightful romp ends with Cleo singing "Now I'm a Lady" as she and Carrington, Earl of Stratford, head off to the *Aquitania* for their honeymoon.

**K**londike Annie (1936) offered Mae the greatest acting challenge of her career. She rose brilliantly to the test, capturing every nuance of the Frisco Doll who moves from the fleshpots of the West to the missions of Nome, Alaska. "She makes the frozen north red hot," shouted the Paramount publicity department in delight. Others were not so pleased. William Randolph Hearst was so outraged about the idea of America's favorite sex symbol as a missionary that he wrote: "Isn't it about time that Congress did something about Mae West?"

The role of Rose Carlton is a radical departure for Mae. First, she walks away from the man she really loves—in this case, handsome Mountie Jack Forrest (Phillip Reed). Of greater interest is the fact that *Klondike Annie* is the only film in which Mae repents for her free and easy life and goes to jail to atone. The usual West fade-out consists of a gay song with Mae on the arm of her well-chosen lover. *Annie* ends in muted fashion with Rose returning to San Francisco to face a prison term.

All this is not to suggest that *Annie* is heavy, dull, or preachy. Mae and director Raoul Walsh keep the pace quick and light. The usual lurid melodramatic touches are present, as are the seemingly endless reserve of Westian innuendos and one-liners.

The film opens in the usual West

# THE SAN FRANCISCO DOLL

fashion: a fancy club—in this case, Chan Lo's elegant eatery in San Francisco's Chinatown. The same eager crowd of men await the evening's star attraction—Mae as Rose Carlton, the San Francisco Doll. Mae's production number is pure inspiration: "I'm an Occidental woman in an Oriental mood for love," she croons, plucking a samisen as Chinese musicians accompany her with bamboo flutes.

The sentiments of Rose's song could hardly be less true. Although she is the white queen of Chinatown, Rose is restless and bored, "caged up here for over a year" she tells her lord and master, Chan Lo (Harold Huber). Chan is a Fu Manchu villain all the way: impenetrable, smooth, and a loquacious bore. To Chan, Rose is the idol of Chinatown, his "white doll," his "pearl of pearls," he drones in what is almost a parody of W.C. Fields in *My Little Chickadee*.

*Rose:* This pearl of pearls is getting unstrung.

*Chan:* It would bring me profoundest sorrow if wings were to carry you to your ancestors.

*KLONDIKE ANNIE (1936). "An Occidental Woman in an Oriental Mood For Love"*

KLONDIKE ANNIE (1936).
With Harold Huber

*KLONDIKE ANNIE (1936). With Victor McLaglen*

*Rose:* You can't say anything the short way, can you?

Rose's aim is to get as far from Chan as possible. This is not an easy matter. Spies lurk behind every lacquered screen, and beneath the club's glossy dining room there is a dark torture chamber. Rose's solution is swift and brutal: during a struggle with Chan, she wrests his prize knife away and does her Chinaman in. Unfortunately this lurid scene was snipped from the final print. Such cuts—and there are others to come—seriously damage the total impact of *Klondike Annie*. Without seeing Rose at her fiercest, the transition to a repentant Bible-toting lady is blunted and unrealistic. Credit Mae's artistry that she convinces us in spite of the cuts.

Our next glimpse of Rose is aboard a ship bound for Alaska. Rose is barely up the gangplank when Captain Bull Brackett (Victor McLaglen) falls head over heels in love with her. Rose treats Bull like dirt but this only serves to inflame his passion. "I'm the captain," Bull announces proudly as Rose saunters aboard. "Glad ya told me," Mae quips as she sweeps by.

In the first heat of infatuation, Bull gives Rose his cabin. "You can use my anteroom for a sitting room or parlor," he grins suggestively. "It'll do," Rose counters, slamming the door in his face. Such tactics only incite Bull, and the next morning we find him serving Rose a lavish breakfast. He hands her a cup of coffee with a spoon:

*Rose:* You do it . . . Stirrin' gets on my nerves.

*Bull:* You certainly are different from any woman I ever bumped into.

*Rose:* Maybe 'cause I'm not in the habit of bein' bumped into . . .

A dash of cream, please . . . Ya mind takin' your feet off mine?

In spite of her antics, Rose is attracted to Bull's virility and his rough-diamond quality. She even gets out her guitar and sings a chorus or two of "Deep Blue Sea, I Hear Ya Callin' Me" for the delighted Bull. Bull has one idea in mind. Mae knows exactly what he wants but for the moment isn't giving.

The turning point in their relationship comes when Bull discovers that Rose is a fugitive from justice. In a fury, Bull turns on her and ac-

*KLONDIKE ANNIE (1936). With Victor McLaglen*

*KLONDIKE ANNIE (1936). With Helen Jerome Eddy*

cuses her of treating him like the "black plague" (which she has). "Ya mighta carved yer name in *my* back," he screams wildly. Rose's technique is pure West: Reclining on a couch in her lavish kimono, *Police Gazette* in hand, she gives him the silent treatment. Finally, when Bull has run out of threats, Rose sneers quietly: "Whaddya gonna do about it?" Like the avenging Chick in *She Done Him Wrong,* Bull soon becomes putty in Rose's hands:

*Bull:* I'd hate to see a rope around that pretty neck.

*Rose:* Don't think it would be very becoming, do you?

*Bull:* Doll, I couldn't give you up if you killed a million guys.

At this point, *Klondike Annie* takes a serious and unexpected turn. On board comes Sister Annie Alden (Helen Jerome Eddy), a prim and proper missionary on her way to Alaska. Bull is livid. How will he get close to Doll if she's sharing her digs with a Bible broad? Rose is a bit worried herself. Gradually, she loosens up, takes Sister Annie in her stride and eventually falls completely under the spell of the woman's missionary zeal. The idea of pairing Mae and a professional do-gooder like Sister Annie is pure inspiration.

Rose offers her new roommate a drink. "Whiskey?" Annie blanches. "Whaddya think it was, sasparilla?," Rose counters.

*Sister Annie:* I'm glad you have the spirit of charity ... It must be hard for a pretty woman like you to be good. You see, sister, I put my whole heart in my work.

*Rose:* So do I. You can always lose your heart but never lose your head.

Though seriously ill with a heart condition, Annie tries to convert Rose and even hands her a Bible. "Pretty thick and the print is pretty small," Mae purrs. "I'll start it tomorrow." The scene ends with a typical West repartee. (Mae always has the last word.)

*Rose:* Oh, you don't snore do you?

*Annie:* Why, I don't know. Do you?

*Rose:* I don't know. I haven't had any complaints.

When Annie falls gravely ill,

*KLONDIKE ANNIE (1936). Rose gets friendly with Bull.*

Rose nurses her unselfishly—but to no avail. Before she expires, Sister Annie bequeaths her Bible to the grief-stricken Rose.

When the ship docks at Nome, the police come on board in search of the fugitive Frisco Doll. Rose is momentarily desperate. Her solution is ingenious. She hastily dresses the corpse in prostitute's garb (another censored scene), then dons Annie's missionary rags. When Rose, now Sister Annie Alden, emerges from her cabin, the expression on the faces of Bull and the police is itself worth the price of admission.

"There's no place like Nome when Mae hits the Yukon!" the Paramount wags promised. And for once, they lived up to their word. Rose moves into the mission with ease and assurance—and for Mae, something new: total commitment. "I gotta debt to pay to Annie," she explains to the dumbstruck Bull who wants her out of Nome and into his bed aboard ship. Rose's dedication to her mission is total and all-consuming.

This does not mean that Mae goes about her business with a long face. Addressing her fellow zealots, she gives preaching a unique touch:

*Rose:* You people've been on the wrong track and I'm gonna steer you right. You'll never get anywhere cause you don't know how to wrassle the devil . . . You gotta know him, know his tricks. I could make him say uncle—that is, if he's got an uncle. I might have to use a little more fireworks than usual.

Rose's tactics are revolutionary and hard-fisted. Her aim is to fill the mission hall on Sunday and nothing is going to stop her. Captain Bull gets a job as hall bouncer—in reverse. He drags the bums *out* of the snow and *into* the meeting. Even local dance hall tarts are pressed into service. "But Sunday's our biggest night," wails the madam. "From now on, it's gonna be *our* biggest night. See you have your girls look their best. They'll be servin' refreshments."

The Sunday night rally is one of the great scenes in any West film, a scene equal in wit and power to her courtroom antics in *I'm No Angel* or the opera ball of *Goin' to Town.* The night is frigid and snowy but inside a barber shop quartet is telling the crowd: "There'll be a hot time in the ole town tonight." The place is bulging with miners, their wives, sweethearts, and tarts. Bull is just kicking in the last recalcitrant drunk when Sister Annie makes her appearance. Whistles, applause, and a standing ovation. Rose gives her "sermon" as a honky-tonk ballad, the usual platitudes emerging as more palatable to her hip-swinging rhythm: "My message comes to you straight from the heart," she begins, then goes

KLONDIKE ANNIE (1936). With Phillip Reed

straight to the heart of her message. "I wanna show ya that ya can think right, do right every day of your lives, and still have a good time in this world." The audience is enchanted.

What wins them over completely is Rose's heart-to-heart talk with a bum who wants only to reform and get back to his little woman. When Rose finishes with him, the women are sniffling and even tough old Bull is hauling out his hankie. The time is ripe for the collection. Brother Ben and Brother David step forward eagerly. Rose takes one look at these two refugees from a Smith Brothers Cough Drop ad and sends Brother Spike and Brother Red—two local winos—to do the task: "Take these, boys," she drawls, passing out the baskets, "and have them filled. Then make a second trip." At the pump organ, Brother Gene plays a toe-tapping version of "Better to Give than· to Receive." The baskets return bulging. The evening is a smash and, like Ruby Carter and Cleo Borden, Rose Carlton has conquered new territories.

With all of this activity, one wouldn't expect Rose to have much time for men. There is no underestimating Mae. Romance appears in the guise of Jack Forrest, a handsome, upright Mountie who is out to capture the Frisco Doll. In a scene pungent with delightful irony, Forrest comes to Sister Annie to find out what *she* knows about the notorious San Francisco entertainer. Business over, Forrest succumbs to Rose's blandishments: "You could do a lot of good if you joined up with us." Forrest takes Rose for a sleigh ride, and deep in the Alaskan forests, they make love. Bull hears about the clandestine meeting and angrily confronts Rose. So now we have the usual West situation: Mae and two jealous lovers. The solution in the past had always been simple: take the better man and no regrets. *Klondike Annie,* however, is different. Mae leaves *both* men and returns to a San Francisco jail to atone. First, however, she must sever her relationship with the mission. With muted violins throbbing "Better to Give than to Receive" on the soundtrack, Rose bids her friends goodbye: "I want ya to build a bigger place and right out in front I want it to say—Sister Annie Alden's Settlement House. *(Under her breath)* Guess she'd kinda like that."

Although her leave-taking is dramatic (and Mae plays the moment extraordinarily well), there are both lurid and comic overtones. Rose's decision to leave Nome has not been purely an act of self-sacrifice. Sashaying down the snowy streets one night for a rendezvous with her Mountie, Mae almost gets a hatchet in her pretty bonnet. She turns quickly to catch a

*KLONDIKE ANNIE (1936). Rose and the Mountie*

pigtail departing into the shadows. Chan Lo's murder will be avenged at all costs. This usual bit of Westian melodrama provokes Mae to choose prison over assassination.

The humor in the situation comes after the fact, so to speak. A woman like Rose in jail? She'll probably charm both jury and judge and end up with everyone securely around her bejeweled little finger. We've already seen her tactics in *I'm No Angel.* Even if Rose does end up in the clink, her special brand of missionary zeal would undoubtedly make it the liveliest of jails.

Even in its somewhat mutilated state, *Klondike Annie* stands as Mae's best film. Walsh's direction is masterful. The story line is strong, full of suspense and local color. Mae's supporting players are superb: McLaglen is all bluster and wounded masculinity; Phillip Reed is polished and urbane in his variation on Paul Cavanagh and Cary Grant, while Helen Jerome Eddy is spinsterly religious zeal personified. Drawing all these diverse elements together is Mae herself—hip-swinging, wise-cracking, blues-singing, Bible-toting, with a rare poignance and depth.

*Go West, Young Man* (1936) is a film rich in comic possibilities. Mae plays Mavis Arden, the "talk of the talkies." The idea is a simple one: take Mavis away from the glamorous world of Hollywood and personal appearance tours and drop her in the midst of a country boarding house. Along the way, there will be ample opportunities to poke fun at Gloria Swanson-type movie queens, small-time politicians, and movie-crazy local yokels.

We are introduced to Mavis (pronounced Mah-viss) during a personal appearance for her latest opus, *Drifting Lady*. The setting is a Washington theater, one of those Roxy-type movie palaces that sprang up all over America in the early thirties. Thousands of eager eyes focus on the stage. The curtains part and out comes Mavis. Against a background of lavish flower baskets, Mavis talks to her public. Her speech is a masterpiece of Westian humor. Mae even gets in a few sly digs at the censor by having Mavis deny her fallen woman screen image. Actually she would rather play a part that expresses "the real me . . . an unaffected country girl that finds her happiness in a garden."

*Mavis:* . . . I'm such a different person really . . . beneath all this glitter, Mavis Arden is a person like yourselves. If you would only come up and see me in my little I-talian

# THE TALK OF THE TALKIES

villa in Hollywood, I'm sure you'd be disappointed in the dullness and simplicity of my life. I know it's cruel to disillusion you this way and you must take this in the right spirit.

Backstage, the corridors are jammed with stage-door Johnnies, all eager for a date with Mavis. Presiding over this hungry mass of silk hats and white ties is Mavis' press agent, Morgan (played with polish and urbanity by Warren William). Morgan's job is to protect the studio's investment: "Her contract won't permit her to marry for five years. My job is to see that she doesn't break that contract." And a tough job it is—complicated by the fact that Morgan is insanely jealous of every Johnnie who admires his difficult quarry.

Morgan's first problem is Francis X. Harrigan (Lyle Talbot), a nobody with political and amorous aspirations. Harrigan sweeps Mavis off to a swank, secluded Washington nightspot. Morgan takes revenge by phoning every newspaper in town and divulging the lovers' hideout. As reporters barge in and flashbulbs pop, Mavis seizes the opportunity to make yet another personal appearance: "Mr.

GO WEST, YOUNG MAN (1936). With Warren William

*GO WEST, YOUNG MAN (1936). With Lyle Talbot*

*GO WEST, YOUNG MAN (1936). With Randolph Scott*

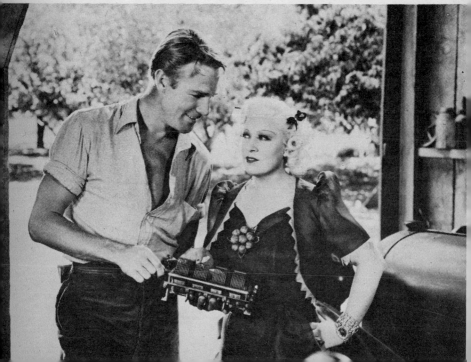

Harrigan and I are just friends, just friends, ain't we honey . . . ah, Mr. Harrigan."

*Reporter:* Have you any political views?

*Mavis* (never at a loss for words): What I think the country needs is more marriage. Millions of lovely girls wasting their lives in factories, shops, offices because millions of men can't afford to marry them. The state should make it possible for them to marry. Endow them as we endow hospitals and colleges. Give every girl a dowry. Provide every couple with a radio and an Italian villa and a baby grand.

Mavis is rightly furious with Morgan for his meddling. Nothing can stop her triumphant series of personal appearances, however, and the next stop is Harrisburg, Pennsylvania. Tooling along the picturesque countryside in her Rolls (Mae's own), garbed in one of Irene Jones' most lavish creations, the inevitable happens—car trouble. Morgan finds help at a gas station run by one of the local yokels. By chance this yokel just happened to be among the eager mob that drooled over Mavis' Washington appearance. Soon the whole countryside is abuzz: "Mavis Arden, the movie star"—the word passes from silo to pigsty. The car, of course,

will need extensive repairs. This means finding a place to put Mavis up.

What transpires now is a delightfully comic reversal of the age-old theme of the country bumpkin who comes to the city to be corrupted. *Go West* gives us the glamorous and powerful (though rather dumb) movie queen who comes from the city and ends up corrupting the entire countryside.

Morgan secures a room at the home of Mrs. Strothers (Alice Brady). Strothers' boarding house is a collection of daffy rural types. First there is the lady herself: proud and once attractive, she is supersensitive about being down on her luck. Daughter Joyce (Margaret Perry) is a languid creature who pouts and sulks about the place. Strothers' Aunt Kate (Elizabeth Patterson) is a flinty old dame who takes one look at Mavis and exclaims: "In my time a woman with hair like that didn't come out in the daytime." Gladys, the maid (Isabel Jewell) is movie crazy, plumb starstruck. Professor Rigby (Etienne Girardot) is a spluttering, crotchety old geezer who tolerates no variations in his daily routine. Completing this odd collection is Nicodemus (Nicodemus Stewart), a Stepin Fetchit black who gets sucked into one of Morgan's most insidious schemes.

In bursts Mavis Arden, movie queen to the tips of her well-

GO WEST, YOUNG MAN (1936). With Randolph Scott

lacquered fingernails. "A ghost'd be willing to haunt this place for nothing," she announces haughtily to Morgan. Then, noting the effect of her tactless remarks on Mrs. Strothers, Mavis moans: "My tragic, tragic temperament . . . why your interior is just as picturesque as your ulterior."

Mavis' first "victim" is Gladys. The promise of an autographed photo sends this screenstruck creature into such a state that she drops the tea dishes. A kind word from Mavis and Gladys is already on her way out to Hollywood. Poor Morgan, in fact, has to sit through Gladys' stultifyingly bad imitation of Marlene Dietrich as the kitchen of the Strothers' homestead momentarily becomes a Berlin cabaret of the twenties. Professor Rigby is so put out by Mavis and all the attention that she is getting that he vows to put this "immoral creature" out. Con-man Morgan calms the old boy down by proposing Rigby as a likely candidate for movie stardom.

The only boarder who doesn't succumb to Mavis is Joyce. And with good reason. Once Mavis has spotted the "large and sinewy" muscles of Joyce's fiancé, Bud Norton, there is no stopping our heroine. The fiancé is none other than Randolph Scott, craggy of profile and brimming over with Huck Finn charm. The scenes between Mae and Scott are the highlights of *Go*

*West, Young Man* and are among the funniest seduction routines ever put on celluloid. Scott plays it straight local yokel, a barnyard Romeo to Mae's vampish movie siren. Certainly Mae has never had so ingenuous a partner upon whom to exert her powerful charms.

Things begin to develop when Mavis discovers that Bud is repairing the Rolls. "Sorry I don't carry spare parts," he remarks, to which Mae, looking him over carefully, counters, "I didn't expect you to." Bud gets carried away with excitement over mechanical things —"puttin' things together and takin' things apart"—but Mae has other things in mind. "It's all pretty technical," he tells her. "I'm afraid you wouldn't understand." Mavis purrs, "You don't know what an understandin' person I can be." What follows is pure gold as Scott attempts to explain his invention. As Scott mumbles about "siloscopes" and "oscillators", Mae undulates and gyrates like the serpent in the Garden of Eden:

*Mavis:* You have beautiful hair for a man . . .

*Bud (gee, shucks, m'am):* Well, I wash it a lot . . . that's the secret.

Phase two of "How to Conquer a Man," by Mavis Arden involves a trip to the shed to see that famous invention. Clusters of grapes dripping bucolically from her bodice, Mavis prepares for her day in the country: "This reminds me of my first picture, *The Farmer's Daughter*. Do you remember? It's a lovely story. I felt very sincere in it." Scott plays right into her willing clutches, as he suggests darkening the room, to her ill-concealed delight.

Mavis is now inclined to take a little walk in the fields. Curled up beside a haystack, Mavis is about to put the make on Bud when nemesis Morgan strikes again. The lovers look up to discover that the whole field is teaming with local citizens and giggling schoolgirls, pens and autograph books in hand. For ten dollars, Morgan had given Nicodemus the starring role of Paul Revere and told him to go and alert the neighbors to the great celebrity in their midst.

Undaunted, Mavis tries again —by moonlight. Bud is toiling on his invention when Mae slinks in dressed for El Morocco. Bud waxes enthusiastic about his oscillator. "I wouldn't be surprised if you'll have to take it to Hollywood," Mavis purrs, then spills out the whole plan to Bud. "I mean to take you to Hollywood myself," she promises.

*GO WEST, YOUNG MAN (1936). With Elizabeth Patterson and Warren William*

GO WEST, YOUNG MAN (1936). With Randolph Scott

Mavis offers meetings with all the big executives, starting undoubtedly with the head of her studio, A. K. Greenfield. Bud is almost beside himself with eager anticipation. Now is the time for the kill.

*Mavis:* You like my perfume. Parlez-moi d'amour . . .

*Bud:* Perfume's a lovely thing but you know they make it outta the durndest things: horses' hooves, potato peels, coal tar . . .

Mavis is undaunted and launches into a torch song: "I was Sayin' to the Moon." "Take a little relaxative," she purrs, trying to lure Bud away from his invention and into a dance.

Once in her arms, Mavis' next weapon is one of the oldest tricks known to the female sex: the "poor little girl who needs a big stranger to take care of her" technique. She enumerates the trappings of her fabulous career, then moans: "What do they count when I've missed the thing that counts most . . . a tender, honest love. If only I could meet someone like . . . *you.*"

*Bud:* I'm nobody ... I haven't got a thing.

*Mavis:* Honey, you've got everything. Look into my eyes and read the truth.

*Bud (carried away by passion—suddenly Gilbert to her Garbo):* Your eyes are like the water in Miller's pond ... gray-brown. Your hair reminds me of corn waving in the sun.

But Bud's raptures are interrupted by Aunt Kate, who shuffles in to listen to her favorite program on the radio. Once again, Mavis is thwarted.

Morgan, ever vigilant, again steps in to foil Mavis. He insinuates that Bud's fiancée Joyce is pregnant. Mavis is shocked enough to bid him a tearful farewell. The scene is pure West, tempered with a twist of Sarah Bernhardt. Mavis starts in low key: "You must be brave, my dear," then goes into gear as she tells the heartsick bumpkin that he must forget her. "Forget that strange October woman who drifted into your life as a summer cloud drifts over a green field, then drifts on again." Certainly an Oscar must be lurking in the wings for such a display—and Mae relishes every moment of her scene.

GO WEST, YOUNG MAN (1936). A climactic moment of confusion

GO WEST, YOUNG MAN (1936). With Lyle Talbot, Randolph Scott and Warren William

*Go West* ends in the usual flurry of melodrama. This time, it's a misunderstanding by politico Harrigan who is still carrying a torch for Mavis. Thinking that she's been kidnapped and dragged off to a sinister boarding house, Harrigan sends police cars and screaming sirens after his lovely quarry. In the ensuing confusion, Morgan gets arrested. Mavis would be only too happy to see him behind bars for all the dirt he's done her. Happy, that is, until she hears him out: "I liked you and thought you had some feeling. Then I liked you even more when I found you didn't." Mavis is momentarily taken aback. Morgan's clever tactics and cool behavior are certainly a perfect match for her headstrong ego.

The fade-out finds the lovers in the back seat of the Rolls. The car is running smoothly now—thanks to Bud. (Is there any justice?) As always, Mae has the last word:

*Morgan:* Your lips were made for kissing.

*Mavis:* That's what I use them for . . .

*Morgan:* From now on there'll be no other men in your life.

*Mavis:* Oh, yeah?

Mae's *Every Day's A Holiday* (1938) runs neck and neck with *The Heat's On* as her worst film. In truth, Mae hadn't wanted the property at all. Her heart was set on playing Russia's Catherine the Great. For years, Mae had been obsessed with a film based on the legendary "Semiramis of the North." Paramount had other plans, however. Producer Emanuel Cohen had some expensive turn-of-the-century sets collecting dust on the back lot. These included, among others, an exact replica of the famed Rectors restaurant. Cohen also had a story line—of sorts. As usual, Mae didn't go for it. She wrote and rewrote to suit her individual needs. The results, alas, are disastrous.

The opening is promising enough: Over the titles and the snappy music, we see fireworks exploding. It is December 31, 1899. The setting is New York. Not the Bowery of Mae's earlier ventures but the Gotham of elegant Fifth Avenue mansions, lavish music halls, and Rectors restaurant, aglitter with chandeliers and wealthy patrons. No longer content with Travis Banton or Irene Jones, Mae hired famed Paris couturiere Elsa Schiaparelli to whip up some astonishing gowns.

Mae plays Peaches O'Day, a con artist whose claim to fame is the thickness of her police record down at City Hall. Peaches' specialty is

## PEACHES AND FIFI

selling the Brooklyn Bridge to unsuspecting immigrants: "When this one wears out, I'll sell ya a new one," she tells a wide-eyed German, just off the boat. Peaches is the special interest of Captain Jim McCarey (Edmund Lowe), a good-looking Irish cop and a paragon of honesty, who would like her to reform.

*Peaches:* I might crack a law now 'n' then, but I ain't never broke one.

*Jim:* The only law you ain't broke is the law of gravity.

*Peaches:* That's an idea. I'll go to work on that right away."

Undaunted by his reprimands, Peaches sashays her way into the elegant Fifth Avenue mansion of Van Reigble van Pelter van Doon, III (Charles Winninger). Van Doon is the bumbling chairman of the Citizens Reform Committee. Peaches twists both van Doon and his butler Graves (Charles Butterworth) around her little finger. Van Doon ends up celebrating New Year's Eve at Rectors, introducing Peaches to high society as his niece from boarding school. Among the guests at Rectors is Nifty Bailey (Walter Catlett), a fast-talking Broadway producer who wants to

100

*EVERY DAY'S A HOLIDAY (1938). As Peaches O'Day*

star Peaches in a revue. Like all small-time producers, Nifty talks a good line but doesn't have a penny. Peaches has a solution: van Doon. And before the old fool smashes up the restaurant in a drunken spree, Peaches gets him to back the show.

There is only one fly in the ointment—honest Captain Mc-Carey. He's got a warrant out for Peaches, and this time he's is taking no chances. He puts Peaches on a boat for Boston with a one-way ticket.

The situation looks grave until Nifty hatches a plan with Peaches: Return to New York not as Peaches O'Day but as Mlle. Fifi, the toast of Gay Paree.

The rest of the plot can be summed up quickly. Fifi becomes the talk of New York (naturally) and the romantic target of corrupt Tammany Hall boss "Honest" John Quade (Lloyd Nolan). Quade is in the first excitement of his upcoming mayoral campaign when he falls head over heels in love with Fifi. Fifi spurns Quade, and Quade, in a rage, orders McCarey to close her show. McCarey refuses and quits. In full battle gear, Fifi makes

*EVERY DAY'S A HOLIDAY (1938). With Edmund Lowe*

*EVERY DAY'S A HOLIDAY (1938). With Walter Catlett*

her assault on City Hall. After demolishing Quade and his office, Peaches-Fifi puts her considerable talents to work backing McCarey for mayor of New York.

Mae's dual role in *Holiday* provides her with ample opportunities to display her wares. She's her usual resourceful, clever, wisecracking self, highly adept at making a fool out of a man. Out on a date with butler Graves, Mae gets him to rob all the goods from a display window. Like Tira cracking her whip, Peaches gets the hapless creature to steal fancy hats and ermine capes. Peaches does a splen-

did job of demolishing poor van Doon: "No woman has crossed my threshold in twenty years," the cantankerous ninny moans. When Peaches bursts into his life, the old gent is completely floored. She takes him for a New Year's Eve joyride at Rectors at which the respectable scion of Dutch ancestors proceeds to become the laughing stock of the place.

Determined to protect her show, Peaches saves her big guns for Honest John Quade. Clad in a black Schiaparelli gown and chinchilla wrap, she leads a fierce black mastiff (wearing matching

*EVERY DAY'S A HOLIDAY* (1938). With Walter Catlett,
Charles Winninger, and Charles Butterworth

*EVERY DAY'S A HOLIDAY (1938). Peaches-Fifi and friends*

accessories) into City Hall. Peaches (Fifi) demands immediate privacy: "Two eeze company, a crowd eeze too much," she purrs suggestively, and Quade immediately sends his boys out to get champagne. Batting her false eyelashes, Fifi comes quickly to the point: "What eeze to become of my bee-utiful show if they close up my theater?" Quade is about to succumb when his fire marshal walks in. Fifi flies into a rage: "How dare you come into my boudoir!" she screams at the bewildered man. "Kick him out."

*Quade:* He's my deputy fire marshal. He has a right to stand there.

*Fifi:* Out! He will stand where I put him.

Mae is the past mistress of the fine art of making a man appear a fool in the eyes of his subordinates. We've already seen her at work on Victor McLaglen and his sailors in

*EVERY DAY'S A HOLIDAY (1938). With Edmund Lowe*

*With Charlie McCarthy and Edgar Bergen on the set of*
*EVERY DAY'S A HOLIDAY*

*Klondike Annie.* The results here are equally devastating. The fire marshal beats a hasty retreat, followed for the moment by Quade. Fifi grabs the opportunity to rifle the files and steal her arrest record. Quade returns, champagne in hand. "Suppose we drink to our future happiness," he grins sheepishly. "Ohhhh, Johneee," Fifi coos seductively, then takes a sip. Her blandishments turn to purple rage as she accuses him of giving her "horreeble vinegar." "Do you not know that I am delicate?," she shrieks.

With this, Fifi proceeds to tear the place apart. Going on a hair-pulling rampage, Fifi climaxes her tirade by posing in the window in the manner of Sarah Bernhardt about to do her "grand emotional scene." Dragging the curtains down about her, Fifi reminisces about her glorious career in Paris. Crying "my gorgeous public eeze waiting for me!," Fifi sweeps out, leaving behind her utter havoc and a thoroughly bewildered and defeated Quade.

Unfortunately, nothing else in this dreary film comes up to Fifi's big moment. The humor is stale and flat: "My what a lovely conversatory," Peaches quips as she enters van Doon's drawing room. Mavis Arden had done it far better back in 1936. Van Doon asks: "Did you ever have a skeleton in your closet?" Peaches: "No, I was always strong and healthy." Van Doon's humor consists mainly of squirting a full bottle of seltzer water in his own bewhiskered face. And so on . . .

When all seems lost, Louis Armstrong comes bouncing and gyrating onto the screen in the big victory parade number that closes the film. Satchmo shouts "Jubilee!" and provides a blast of excitement and infectious energy that the film sorely needs. Stealing a leaf from Cleo Borden's book, Peaches has vowed to "put on a show that'll make Barnum & Bailey look like a flea circus." Resplendent and bejeweled, Peaches is the star of the parade as she beats the drums in her carriage. The crowd applauds her election speech for McCarey: "Folks, you can't go wrong with McCarey. I found that out. He's just the kind of a man you want . . . at least he's the kind of man I want . . . for mayor, I mean." Mae beats her drums, Louis blasts his trumpet, and the film draws to its roaring close.

With *Holiday* under her belt, Mae returned to her dream—a lavish color film to be called *Catherine Was Great*. Paramount was still not interested and so they released Mae from her contract. At this point Universal approached Mae with a proposal to make a picture with W. C. Fields. Mae accepted. What followed was the stormy collaboration that produced *My Little Chickadee* (1940).

At first glance, the idea of a partnership between the misanthropic Fields and the wisecracking West seemed a publicist's dream. From the documents collected in *W. C. Fields by Himself* (edited by his grandson), we learn that Fields was delighted at the prospect of working with Mae and proceeded to prepare scenario after scenario. Fields' letters show just how eager he was to get the project off the ground: "Miss West has only to wave her little finger," he wrote on September 11, 1939, "to have me pitch in and write scenes for her or collaborate with her or leave her entirely alone, as she desires."

Mae also pitched in: "I did my best to make Bill Fields' scenes as funny as possible. He was pleased with most of them, though he insisted on putting in some of his fine character touches—which were no more than I would have done in his place." Mae's major complaint was

# FLOWER BELLE MEETS CUTHBERT J. TWILLIE

a bartending sequence which came to some four pages of dialogue: "None of it had anything to do with the story or plot of the picture."

Fields' drinking problem was well known in Hollywood so that Mae had a stringent "no liquor on the set" clause written into her own contract. Fields, however, found ways to get around this, even, Mae reports, to bringing the booze in a Coke bottle. Mae was also disturbed at his clowning on the set. One day she found Fields telling a group of child performers to "go play out in the traffic." Years later, Mae summed up the situation as follows: "Some people have gotten the quaint idea that I made more than one film with W.C. Fields—no way, baby, one was enough."

*My Little Chickadee* follows what is by now an almost inflexible West pattern: Mae surrounded by two men—one a boorish fool she treats with utter contempt; the other, an honest, upstanding and, of course, handsome type who wants only to reform her. In *Annie*, Mae had been courted by oafish Victor McLaglen and desired by honest Mountie Phillip Reed. In *Holiday*, Lloyd Nolan stepped into McLag-

MY LITTLE CHICKADEE (1940). On the set with W. C. Fields

len's big shoes while Edmund Lowe personified honesty and the law. In *Chickadee,* Mae is Flower Belle Lee, courted by snake-oil salesman Fields and adored by crusading newspaperman Wayne Carter (Dick Foran). For variety, Mae throws in Joseph Calleia who doubles as a corrupt saloon keeper by day and an amorous masked rider by night. This, too, is familiar. The saloon keeper is akin to Gus Jordan in *She Done Him Wrong* or Buck Gonzales in *Goin' to Town.* The masked rider is simply a smarter version of Roger Pryor about to steal Ruby Carter's diamonds.

These patterns aside, *Chickadee* is strictly a West-Fields co-starring vehicle. On the eve of World War II, the moviegoing public paid its money to see two of the most celebrated comic talents of the day. And neither they nor the thousands who have lined up since were disappointed.

Mae's Flower Belle is a loose woman who gets run out of town. Flower Belle, it seems, was abducted one day by a mysterious masked rider. Brought back to safety, Flower Belle was apparently so pleased with her adventure that the indignant townswomen, led by the overbearingly righteous Margaret Hamilton, banish her from the community.

Fields plays Cuthbert J. Twillie,

MY LITTLE CHICKADEE (1940). The courtship of Cuthbert
J. Twillie

Getting better acquainted with Flower Belle

Whispering words of endearment

con man and snake-oil salesman. We first meet Twillie as he is being pulled on a sled across the prairie by his trusty Indian. Fields blocks the oncoming train, boards it, and discovers Flower Belle. The fun is on.

In her candid volume of reminiscences, *W.C. Fields and Me,* Carlotta Monti quotes the Master's cardinal rules of comedy:

1. Never break anything.
2. A henpecked husband gets surefire laughs.
3. Clothes are of paramount importance: "every crease, fold and droop of flesh can be the object of hilarity."
4. Everyone has a percentage of the sadist in him.

The scenes between West and Fields provide the student of comedy with ample proof of the rules. Stovepipe hat atop his head, bulbous nose glowing, carpetbag bulging with money, Twillie spots Flower Belle on the train: "Who is that vision of loveliness up there?", he coos in that inimitable twang. Mae continues buffing her nails.

*Twillie:* Nice day . . . may I present my card?

*Flower Belle:* Novelties and notions? What kinda notions ya got?

*Twillie:* You'd be surprised. Some are old. Some are new.

Flower Belle . . . what a euphonious appellation, easy on the ears and a banquet for the eyes.

*Flower Belle:* You're kinda cute yourself.

*Twillie:* Thank you, I never argue with a lady.

*Flower Belle:* Smart guy.

Taking her hand, Twillie asks if he might kiss her "symmetrical digits," and even wonders if he might "avail" himself of a "second helping." When he presents her with "a little amulet" he received from the Aga Kahn, Twillie senses she is softening:

*Twillie:* It's not fun for a man to be alone.

*Flower Belle:* No fun for a woman either.

*Twillie:* Is it possible for us to be lonesome together?

*Flower Belle:* Quite possible . . .

*Twillie:* I will be all things to you—father, mother, husband, counselor, *(a twinkle in his eye)* . . . bartender . . .

*Flower Belle (eyeing his bulging carpet bag):* You're offering quite a bundle . . .

*Twillie:* My heart is a bargain today. Will you take me?

*Flower Belle:* I'll take ya and

*MY LITTLE CHICKADEE (1940). Two-gun Flower Belle.*
*Fainted lady: Margaret Hamilton*

how. *(With a glance at chaperone Margaret Hamilton.)* It certainly pays to be a good woman.

Twillie is about to seal their bargain with a kiss when there is a whoop and a battle cry offscreen. Indians! Twillie gets out his slingshot, while Flower Belle continues with her nails. When an arrow whizzes by, just missing her fancy bonnet, Flower Belle doesn't bat an eyelash. Twillie is having the time of his life: "It's a regular shootin' gallery!", he shouts as another Indian bites the dust. Joining in the fun, Flower Belle whips out her pistols and proceeds to diminish the tribe with the accuracy of a born sharpshooter. When the screen is nothing but a mass of Indian bodies, Flower Belle packs up her guns and quips: "I almost broke one of ma fingernails."

As the dust settles, Twillie and Belle are "married" by a local card shark, doubling as a minister: "Of course you both know the rules of the game." Hamilton weeps copious tears as her charge finally becomes an honest woman.

Greasewood City is the destination, and here the fun really gets going. Loaded down with luggage, the hapless Twillie trudges behind Flower Belle to the local hotel. There are just two rooms left. "I'll take the honeymoon suite, give him the room," she drawls, slamming the door in Twillie's face. Twillie

MY LITTLE CHICKADEE (1940). With Ruth Donnelly and Fuzzy Knight

*MY LITTLE CHICKADEE (1940). With Dick Foran*

tries charm: "My doll . . . my little doll pie . . . my rose petal . . . my little sugar-coated wedding cake," he coos. The door stays locked. He returns with a phony telegram: "Slip it under the door," comes the sharp order.

Twillie finally does make it in and the resultant scene is 40 percent West, 40 percent Fields, and 20 percent *Midsummer Night's Dream.* With thoughts of that honeymoon uppermost in his mind, Twillie sets about preparing himself for the joyous occasion:

*Twillie:* With your permission I shall dunk my pink and white body in yonder Roman tub. It is with regret that I leave you even to bathe.

*Flower Belle:* Don't forget to take your gloves off.

*Twillie (in expectant ecstasy):* Yum . . . yum . . .

Mae now prepares her prize trick. She puts a goat under the bedclothes with special orders: "Keep

117

*MY LITTLE CHICKADEE (1940). Flower Belle teaches a lesson.*

*THE HEAT'S ON (1943). With Victor Moore*

your mouth closed and let him do all the talkin'. If you do this right, I'll get you one of his straw hats."

Mae slips off to the saloon and the camera now pans to the lavish bathroom. Fields is inspecting the place. A bottle of perfume catches his eye. He takes a big swig. ("That old reprobate would drink a cup of hemlock if it had an olive in it," Gene Fowler once remarked of Fields.) Sporting Flower Belle's frilliest nightie, Twillie prepares his assault. Rubbing his hands and murmuring "my love dove," he climbs into bed. A whinney. Then another. "The sweet little dear is calling for her mother. What sublime innocence!"

Twillie makes one more try to consummate his "marriage." Disguised as that mysterious masked rider, he climbs a ladder to Flower Belle's suite. One glance at that famous red nose and one whiff of breath tells Mae all: "Whaddya been drinkin', embalmin' fluid?," she counters and shoves Twillie —ladder and all—out the window.

No West film is complete without the upright, handsome leading man. In this case, it is Dick Foran as Wayne Carter, Greasewood City's crusading newspaperman. Carter is an idealist, but before long, he is captivated by Flower Belle:

*Carter:* I think you could turn a man's head very early if he wasn't careful.

*Flower Belle:* There's no fun in bein' too careful.

*Carter:* Ain't you forgettin' that you're married?

*Flower Belle:* I'll do my best.

*Carter (feeding her):* Spring is the time for love.

*Flower Belle:* Whatsamatter with the rest of the year?

*Carter:* I don't like to see a girl like you go into bars. They're sordid and full of temptation.

*Flower Belle (fixing him with the famous West stare):* I generally avoid temptation unless I can't resist it.

Carter invites Flower Belle to the local schoolhouse. The visit provides Mae with her "set piece," without which no West film is complete. *Chickadee* is the first film since *Night after Night* in which Mae doesn't have a big musical production number. She makes up for this with a "personal appearance" for Carter in the schoolroom.

Carter explains that the regular teacher has fled into hiding after the local yokels gave her a hard time. No one gives Mae a hard time and her first act as teacher is to crack the whip: "Stand up . . . sit down . . . this is your first lesson in discipline!" The children obey, mouths hanging open. Soon she is into teaching them her own version of history ("Cleopatra . . . fooled around with snakes. Those snakes didn't rattle . . . they swooned.") or mathematics ("Two and two is four and five'll get ya ten if ya know how to work it.") Subtraction is easy: "A man has a hundred dollars. You leave him with two." The Gospel According to Mae.

The finale of *My Little Chickadee* offers a few new twists. Instead of sauntering to the altar or sailing on an ocean cruiser with the man of the hour, Mae is left with two choices: honest newspaperman or the "unmasked" masked rider. Flower Belle looks from one eager face to the other: "I gotta think it over but don't let that keep ya from comin' around." There is still Twillie to be disposed of before the fade. Carpetbag in hand, Fields doffs his hat politely:

*Twillie:* You must come up 'n' see me sometime.

*Flower Belle:* I'll do that, my little chickadee . . .

The camera pans to Mae's derrière as she escorts Fields out of town—"The End."

*My Little Chickadee* was Mae's

*THE HEAT'S ON (1943). With Victor Moore and William Gaxton*

THE HEAT'S ON (1943). Mae in the "Hello, My Amigo" number

last film for three years, and when she returned in Columbia's *The Heat's On* in the fall of 1943, it was unfortunately a disastrous occasion. The critics outdid themselves in heaping scorn upon the film. Here are a few typical quotes: "If this is the best that Mae West can do, brother, it's not so hot!" "The heat is not only on but the radiators are stone cold and the tenants are yelling for the janitor." "Turkeys run rampant on Broadway," declared *PM*, while the cruelest cut of all came from the *New York Daily News* which noted that "Miss West is outclassed by a cute trick in Xavier Cugat's orchestra."

As a production, *The Heat's On* was doomed from the start. Gregory Ratoff, who had co-starred with Mae in *I'm No Angel*, approached her with an adaptation of a Broadway musical called *Tropicana*. Mae liked Ratoff's "borscht and sour cream personality" *and* his idea and gave her verbal commitment. Weeks later, Ratoff returned with a completely different story. "From a writer's standpoint, it was nothing but a hodgepodge of banal situations,"

Mae noted. During his time away, Ratoff had shot some advance footage and now everything was in readiness for the star. The situation was further complicated by the fact that the bank had financed the entire venture on the strength of Mae West's record at the box office.

Always careful of her professional image, Mae feared bad publicity. She reluctantly agreed to go ahead on the production on condition that she write her own scenes. The final product, according to Mae, was "dismal." Then and there she made a firm resolve: "I would never do another picture unless everything but everything was to my satisfaction and so stipulated in black and white."

*The Heat's On* is hardly worth discussing except to note that Mae appears as a high-powered and temperamental Broadway star who is involved with Broadway veterans William Gaxton and Victor Moore in a series of confusing and lackluster plot complications. The musical numbers with Cugat are up to Mae's own lavish standards but it is pianist-singer Hazel Scott, tickling the keys of a battered old upright, who all but steals the show. Mae looks good in the picture— very good indeed for all of her fifty-two years. In fact, there is a marked resemblance to a sexy young lady named Betty Grable who had become the darling of the GI's only a few years before in *Down Argentine Way*.

*Aboard the Queen Mary in 1954.*

Mae had been absent from the screen for almost thirty years when she was offered and delightedly accepted the role of Letitia van Allen in the film version of Gore Vidal's bestselling *Myra Breckenridge* (1970). In the final cut, Mae's role is little more than a cameo. Nonetheless, she received her usual star salary and top billing.

What had she been doing all the years since *The Heat's On?* Never one for long periods of inactivity, Mae had filled her life with Broadway shows (*Catherine Was Great,* among them), a triumphant London season as *Diamond Lil,* and a record-breaking nightclub act. To be sure, there were film offers—dozens of them. Among the more tantalizing were two bids from Federico Fellini to play in *Juliet of the Spirits* and his later *Satyricon.* Mae obviously wasn't eager for a trip to Italy. She also decided not to step in when Marlene Dietrich bowed out of *Pal Joey.* Playing Elvis Presley's mother in *Roustabout* seemed more her style but that, too, didn't pan out.

When *Myra Breckenridge* came along, Mae was ready and willing: "Mr. Vidal writes with beautiful descriptive prose, achieving masterly characterizations—he has an irony and wit that makes for fascinating reading." Some literary critics failed to share her enthusiasm for the novel, while others con-

# LETITIA VAN ALLEN: MEN CLIENTS ONLY

curred wholeheartedly. But it was commonly agreed that, within the space of nearly three hundred pages, Vidal had managed to satirize everything from movie-mad transsexuals to corrupt California judges. His hero-heroine is the implacable Myra, "who no man will ever possess," and whose beauty is nothing less than blinding. When such a creature hits Hollywood, the results could not be anything less than cataclysmic.

Myra's Hollywood sidekick is Letitia van Allen, the most powerful agent (and woman) in town, the "Semiramis of the West," The Catherine the Great of Hollywood and Vine. Letitia's casting couch has held "just about every stud in town who wants to be an actor." Letitia is insatiable and ruthless, the Queen Bee incarnate. In short, the ideal role for Mae's return to the screen.

The finished product, however, was a mess—a disaster for all concerned. Mae didn't get along with Raquel Welch. Producer Robert Fryer was clearly unhappy with director Michael Sarne. Mae was also upset about Sarne's lighting and some of his camera angles. Her "movie queen" manner didn't set well with Sarne. Sarne decided to

*MYRA BRECKENRIDGE (1970). As Letitia van Allen*

show Mae who was boss, and she has described the results in rather polite terms: "I do believe the film was damaged by Sarne's editing out some of my scenes and failing to shoot others I had written. Sarne upset the story line by injecting elements that disturbed, confused or irritated the movie-goer." Mild words for the finished product. Sarne tries desperately to be off-beat, kinky, and perverse—but the result is merely puerile and tasteless.

Consider the opening scene: We are in a hospital operating room, or is it a murky torture chamber from the Dark Ages? A vast audience is assembled. Myron Breckenridge (played in surly fashion by Rex Reed) is about to become Myra. The surgeon enters, maniacally waving a meat cleaver. "Wish me luck," he leers at the nurses. The deed is done, and the audience applauds vigorously. Shirley Temple flashes on the screen singing "You've got to S-M-I-L-E" and suddenly it's kiddie matinée time.

Sarne is not content merely to satirize the Hollywood pop culture. All America is on trial. When a hippie is beaten up by the L.A. police—right outside Schwab's

*MYRA BRECKENRIDGE (1970). With John Huston, Raquel Welch, and Rex Reed*

*MYRA BRECKENRIDGE (1970). With Raquel Welch*

*MYRA BRECKENRIDGE (1970). As Letitia van Allen*

Drugstore—the soundtrack throbs with "America, I Love You." The judge who interrogates Rusty (Roger Herren), Myra's "prize" student, is as slippery as they come. He boldly proclaims the supremacy of the National Rifle Association, openly takes bribes, and keeps his grass stashed away between the covers of *Blackstone's Law Commentaries.*

Sarne's Hollywood is an absolute Disneyland of perversity: transsexualism, orgies, beatings in the streets, drug busts, etcetera. The central symbol is Buck Loner's Academy, a thinly disguised brothel where Buck (John Huston) —a former Western star—presides over the nation's dregs and misfits. Buck spends most of his time on the massage table as a veritable United Nations of comely ladies officiates over him. "Can you take the heartache and the torture and the heat of the five kilowatt bulbs at MGM?," Buck growls, as his way-out faculty prepares the future "greats" of the silver screen. When they're not engaged in making porno flicks, the students hang out at one orgy or another.

It is time for Myra. An atomic blast fills the screen: "My purpose in coming to Hollywood is the destruction of the American male in all its particulars." In this case, one special American male, a stud named Rusty, who ends up on the other end of Myra's two-foot dildo. Myra fits perfectly into the academy. Sporting a sailor suit, she regales her eager students with the glories of forties' films and sex, American style. In truth, Raquel Welch copes as well as can be expected with the transsexual Myra, even revealing some rather subtle comic touches previously untapped in her prehistoric-woman epics.

The stage is set for Mae's arrival. The soundtrack throbs to the beat of "Has Anybody Seen My Gal?" An enormous Rolls-Royce (Mae's own) tools through the streets of Hollywood, *two* chauffeurs at the wheel. The scene switches to a glass office skyscraper. The sign on the door announces boldly: "Letitia van Allen—Men Clients Only." "Miss van Allen is on her way up!" the flagrantly gay secretary trills, all the while blowing kisses at the male applicants who are eagerly forming a double line.

"I'll be right with you, boys. Get your resumés out." Then to the secretary: "I'm a little tired today. One of those guys'll have to go." Catherine the Great, indeed.

Letitia's initial applicant is the "hunkiest" number of the bunch. His first view of the "inner office" is a stunner: a huge chandelier glitters brightly, the place is swathed in white satin, puffed and draped in elegant Austrian style—fringes, tassels, and scallops. Letitia gets

*MYRA BRECKENRIDGE (1970). Letitia in her office*

At the New York premiere of MYRA BRECKENRIDGE

right down to business.

*Letitia:* I don't care about your credits as long as you're oversexed.

*Stud:* That's one of my credits. I never did see a bed in an office before.

*Letitia:* I do a lotta night work.

It's Mae up to her old tricks, to be sure. But now she's commanding, not inviting, and the men are the no-talents of Hollywood. No longer is it fun to banter with the likes of Cary Grant or Paul Cavanagh. Now it's strictly business. At this crucial point, Sarne introduces a tasteless piece of unnecessary comedy. Larry, of the Three Stooges, crosses the screen from left to right dragging a twelve-foot pole. As fellow Stooge Moe watches in wonderment, Larry drags the pole back—from right to left. The joke is crude and obvious. For seventy years Mae had been getting laughs by suggestion and insinuation. She didn't need this.

Following the depressing spectacle of Mae indulging in more "interviews," we next see her back on the boulevards of Hollywood. Regally ensconced in her Rolls, she is accompanied by several motorcycle cops. (Letitia seems to have her own private police force. After all, Catherine the Great had her strapping palace guards.) Letitia takes out her mirror and notices a car in hot pursuit.

*Policeman:* Want me to bust him?

*Letitia:* No! Introduce him . . . Don't forget to remind me of the policeman's balls . . . I mean the police show . . .

This shabby little exchange is far below Mae at her best. Could it be that she was finally getting her revenge on the censors for emasculating her best thirties films?

Mae's next appearance is essentially the first scene all over again—with new studs. There is the same entrance between the double line of males and the same quips: "I'll be right with ya, boys. There's enough for all of ya." The added novelty is a frantic Italian gigolo who waves a letter of introduction from the "great Italian director Federico Fellini." Extricating herself from his mad embraces ("When Mario makes love, the birds sing"), Letitia quips: "You're the wildest salesman since Columbus." Then, to her secretary: "Get a test on this guy." Secretary: "A screen test?" Letitia: "No, a blood test."

Mae's big scene in *Myra* is her visit to Buck Loner's Academy. Mae obviously loved playing with John Huston. In her autobiography she notes: "He set a pace in his scenes that swept *Myra* along in a fast tempo." "There're no more studs anymore," Letitia complains to Buck and the ever-attentive

Myra. "Everyone's popping pills and smokin' grass." Talk turns to Rusty's recent drug bust. "I'll take care of that," Letitia vows. "I have a judge by the ———!" Mae emphasizes her point with a hand gesture. Before she leaves, Letitia indicates a pair of male twins sitting at a nearby table. "I'm the only one who knows the difference," she quips in a momentary flash of the old West brilliance.

No Mae West film would be complete without her big production number and *Myra Breckenridge* is no exception. Sporting a salmon-colored gown and surrounded by a bevy of black chorus boys, Mae croons "Ya Gotta Taste All the Fruit." Sarne's avenging hand is everywhere apparent in this scene. The song itself is preceded by the famous giant banana routine from Busby Berkeley's *The Gang's All Here.* (One thing Mae has never needed is a boost from anyone else.) Sarne further compounds matters by switching the camera away from Mae during her song and focusing on a dull morality discussion led by Myra and attended by Rusty and his girlfriend Mary-Ann (Farrah Fawcett).

Our final view of Mae is the most depressing of all. Myra is in bed with Mary-Ann. The phone rings. It is Letitia. The camera pans to her bedroom. Rusty is spread out on Letitia's bed in a crucifix position—obviously spent. Letitia is ecstatic in her praise of the boy. Myra is deliberately vague so as not to let Mary-Ann know where Rusty is:

*Myra:* Is it the right color?

*Letitia:* Well I guess so. It's the usual color. Didn't you ever make it with him?

*Myra:* I hope he sleeps well in his new home.

This bit of salaciousness playing on the ambiguity of "it" is bottom-drawer West.

Whatever the reasons for Mae's behavior in *Myra Breckenridge,* she emerges as a sad parody of a sex queen, uttering pale copies of the snappy lines that delighted millions of movie-goers and became part of our national folk heritage.

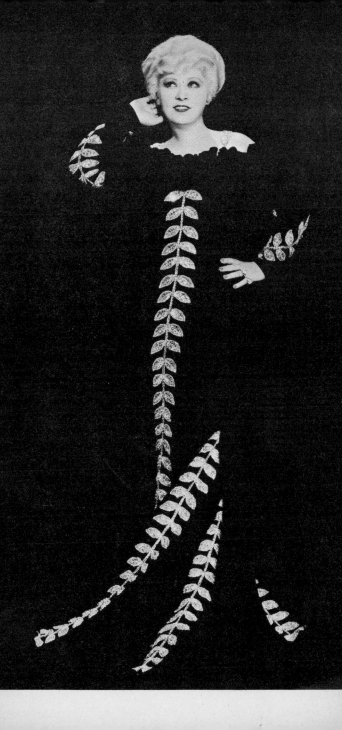

"It wasn't what I did but how I did it," Mae once remarked. And she could not have been more right. The dawn of the Westian age brought an entirely new attitude towards sex on the silver screen. Before Mae, the Hollywood siren had been heavy and sinister, a wench in spangles or clinging black velvet gown who lured men to their doom. With Mae, sex became breezy and humorous, a light-hearted activity without guilt, recriminations, or emotional involvement of any kind. Mae had a quality that no other vamp had even considered: the rare ability to laugh at herself. No matter how tough or manipulative she got, there was always a self-mocking smile ready to flicker beneath that famous sneer.

She was also clearly the superior of the men who threw themselves so recklessly at her feet: "I'm the woman's ego ... I dominate the men in my pictures ... I once looked around and saw that men could go out and do everything they wanted sexually. The more their conquests, the more medals were pinned on them. If a woman took one false step, she was ruined forever. I decided this was nonsense." Herein lies Mae's true uniqueness, and her special niche in the annals of feminism.

To be sure, other women stars of the time—Rosalind Russell, Claudette Colbert, and Irene Dunne, among them—often took

# LIBERATED MAE

strong feminist stands. Unlike Mae, however, these broad-shouldered ladies usually sputtered and fumed about their independence, only to end up in the final reel in the arms of Melvyn Douglas or Fred MacMurray. At the same time that Mae, in *Goin' to Town*, was boldly exchanging suggestive banter with Paul Cavanagh and brazenly taking up with the men of Buenos Aires and Long Island society, Claudette Colbert, in *She Married Her Boss*, was willingly giving up a career for love and marriage with Melvyn Douglas. A high-powered executive secretary with a bright future, Colbert reprimands a colleague who admires her career. "Sit in the moonlight and hold hands," she advises. "A career leaves you empty. Do something important." Mae would have given her a scornful glance and remarked, as she does in *She Done Him Wrong*, "Diamonds is my career."

Mae's humorously frank attitude toward men-women relationships remained the exception rather than the rule through the balance of the thirties and well into the forties as dozens of "boss-ladies" expressed their independence and self-reliance, then tumbled into teary confessions of wanting to be nothing more than compliant wives

*SHE DONE HIM WRONG (1933). With Cary Grant*

I'M NO ANGEL (1933). As Tira

*I'M NO ANGEL (1933). Tira addresses the jury.*

and mothers. In *Honeymoon in Bali* (1939), for example, Madeleine Carroll flexes her muscles as the powerful head of a department store, until romance beckons in the guise of Fred MacMurray. When a long-patient suitor tells her, "Your kind of boss-woman needs a boss-man," Carroll finally agrees, and by the end of the movie, she is on her honeymoon in Bali with MacMurray. ("A husband and children are necessary to make me complete.") Again, Mae would have curled her lip in outrage. Marriage, she tells an ardent swain in *I'm No Angel*, is only "a last resort."

The thirties movie heroine who perhaps came closest to sharing Mae's liberated views, only to surrender to the blandishments of romance, was Theodora Lynn (Irene Dunne) in Columbia's 1936 comedy, *Theodora Goes Wild*. Theodora is a modest, rather mousey small-town girl who lives with her two maiden aunts. However, she has a surprising secret: under a pseudonym she has authored the season's sexiest, most scandalous novel. The film moves from the cloistered atmosphere of Lynnfield, Connecticut to the New York jungle where Theodora meets commercial artist Michael Grant (Melvyn Douglas). Michael advises the girl to "step out and be yourself." Theodora takes Michael at his word and soon finds herself

addressing women's conclaves in terms that today's Women's Liberation movement would approve: "I say this to the modern young girl — be free — express yourself. Take your life in your hands and mold it." A myriad of plot complications leads, nonetheless, to the movie's inevitable conclusion: Theodora in the arms of Michael, her rebellion behind her. Mae would have won her man—and then written an even more scandalous novel.

Liberated ladies all—that is, until the final reel. But not Mae. She didn't want to melt in anyone's arms. She wanted to do the melting herself. (In *I'm No Angel*, she tells an enslaved Cary Grant, "I did my best to make you that way.") Her cheerfully aggressive sexual behavior was in startling contrast to the behavior of all other movie heroines, who could be impudent and sassy but who were expected to remain demure as well. In *Easy Living* (1937), Jean Arthur could find herself in a compromising position—living in a lavish hotel suite rented by tycoon Edward Arnold—but she is only an innocent pawn in a comic misunderstanding and even winds up marrying Arnold's son, Ray Milland. Mae would have parried both father and son with joyful ease. And in *Hands Across the Table* (1935), Carole Lombard shares an apartment with Fred MacMurray,

*BELLE OF THE NINETIES (1934). With John Mack Brown*

GOIN' TO TOWN (1935). Cleo and the hounds

*GOIN' TO TOWN (1935). Cleo and the jockey set*

and when he becomes amorous, she pushes him away firmly. When she agrees to tuck him into bed, he murmurs, "You're as good as my mother was. Mother used to kiss me goodnight." Lombard replies, "I'm *almost* as good as your mother was." With a wisecrack and a leer, Mae would have been more receptive.

As for being a "liberated" woman, Mae never wanted to be equal to men. She always knew that she was *better* than men: a fourteen-carat diamond among swine who could be easily dominated. ("Some of the wildest men make the best pets," she tells John Miljan in *Belle of the Nineties*.) She mocked men by exaggerating all the female characteristics they were supposed to drool over. And she got what she wanted by playing their game, and playing it with a good-natured sneer behind that tough exterior and that undulating walk. Mae always has the last few words, and these words, more often than not, are "Oh, yeah?"

\* \* \* \* \*

"What do you want to be remembered for?," an avid reporter asked Mae recently. Her answer was immediate and characteristic: "Everything." And the lady might just get her wish. Her screen image is unquestionably unique: the marcelled hair, the full bosom, the voluptuously wide hips that caused Truman Capote to dub her the "Big Ben of the hourglass figure," the sashay of a walk, the mouth full of a seemingly endless supply of wisecracks and innuendos.

One of Mae's quips might well sum up her entire remarkable career: "Too much of a good thing can be wonderful." The lady has always been exceptional—and well aware of her uniqueness. "I hold records all over the world . . . that's my ego, breaking records." Barely out of her teens, Mae was writing and acting in her own vaudeville skits. At age twenty-six, she penned a Broadway show called *Sex*, starred in it, promoted it, and even went to jail for it. The transition from Broadway to Hollywood was equally glittering. Mae's films —eight of which she wrote herself—became boxoffice sensations all over the world. One— *She Done Him Wrong*— singlehandedly saved Paramount from going under during the darkest days of the Depression. When Mae took to radio, the results were devastating. Her single appearance on the Charlie McCarthy-Edgar Bergen show provoked such howls of outrage that NBC banned her name from the airwaves. During World War II, Mae became an international household word when British airmen named their inflatable life preservers after a rather prominent part of her famous anatomy. When her film career

*GOIN' TO TOWN (1935). With Ivan Lebedeff, Monroe Owsley, and Tito Coral*

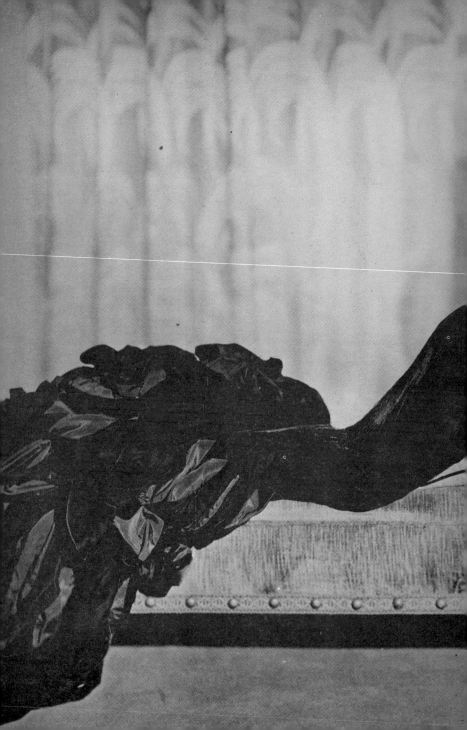

began to ebb after the war, Mae dusted off *Diamond Lil* and polished it to such a degree that she got another four years of mileage out of the old girl—on *both* sides of the Atlantic. Three years of musclemen in posh nightclubs followed. Then a bestselling autobiography and a controversial return to the screen in *Myra Breckenridge* . . . .

Now, well into her eighth decade, Mae is still preaching a gospel of sex and liberation. She has written a novel called *Pleasure Man* and a tome on "sex, health, and the occult"—a subject she knows more about than almost anybody. After that there will probably be another film. A color remake of *She Done Him Wrong?* Well, perhaps, if George Cukor lives long enough to direct it. If not, there will always be some project to engage her insatiably creative ego.

And after that . . . well, knowing Mae, she will probably be reincarnated as the sex symbol of the twenty-first century . . . .

# BIBLIOGRAPHY

*Books*

Fields, Ronald J. editor. *W.C. Fields by Himself.* Prentice-Hall, Englewood Cliffs, New Jersey, 1973.
Monti, Carlotta. *W.C. Fields and Me.* Warner Paperback Library, New York, 1973.
Parish, James Robert. *The Paramount Pretties.* Arlington House, New Rochelle,New York, 1972.
Tuska, Jon. *The Films of Mae West.* Citadel, Secaucus, New Jersey, 1973.
Vidal, Gore. *Myra Breckenridge.* Bantam Books, New York, 1968.
West, Mae. *Goodness Had Nothing to Do With It.* MacFadden Books, New York, 1970.
Yablonsky, Lewis. *George Raft.* McGraw-Hill, New York, 1974.

*Periodicals*

Meryman, Richard. "Interview," *Life,* April 18, 1969.
"The Queen at Home in Hollywood." *Interview,* Vol. 4, No. 12, December 1974.
West, Mae. "Sex in the Theater." *Parade,* Vol. 1, September, 1929.
West, Mae. "Interview." *Take One,* Vol. 4, No. 1, September-October, 1972.

151

# THE FILMS OF MAE WEST

*The director's name follows the release date. Sp indicates screenplay and b/o indicates based/on.*

1.  NIGHT AFTER NIGHT. Paramount. 1932. *Archie Mayo.* Sp: Vincent Lawrence and Kathryn Scola. Cast: George Raft, Constance Cummings, Wynne Gibson, Alison Skipworth, Roscoe Karns, Louis Calhern.

2.  SHE DONE HIM WRONG. Paramount. 1933. *Lowell Sherman.* Sp: Harvey Thew and John Bright, b/o play by Mae West. Cast: Cary Grant, Owen Moore, Gilbert Roland, Noah Beery, Sr., Rafaela Ottiano, Rochelle Hudson, David Landau.

3.  I'M NO ANGEL. Paramount. 1933. *Wesley Ruggles.* Sp: Mae West, b/o her story. Cast: Cary Grant, Gregory Ratoff, Edward Arnold, Kent Taylor, Gertrude Michael, William B. Davidson, Libby Taylor, Dorothy Peterson.

4.  BELLE OF THE NINETIES. Paramount. 1934. *Leo McCarey.* Sp: Mae West, b/o her story. Cast: Roger Pryor, John Mack Brown, John Miljan, Katherine DeMille, James Donlan, Libby Taylor, Gene Austin, Duke Ellington and his orchestra.

5.  GOIN' TO TOWN. Paramount. 1935. *Alexander Hall.* Sp: Mae West, b/o story by Marion Morgan and George B. Dowell. Cast: Paul Cavanagh, Gilbert Emery, Marjorie Gateson, Tito Coral, Ivan Lebedeff, Fred Kohler, Sr., Monroe Owsley, Luis Alberni.

6.  KLONDIKE ANNIE. Paramount. 1936. *Raoul Walsh.* Sp: Mae West, b/o play by Mae West and story by Marion Morgan and George B. Dowell. Cast: Victor McLaglen, Phillip Reed, Helen Jerome Eddy, Harold Huber, Soo Yong, Lucille Webster Gleason.

7.  GO WEST, YOUNG MAN. Paramount. 1936. *Henry Hathaway.* Sp: Mae West, b/o play by Lawrence Riley. Cast: Warren William, Randolph Scott, Alice Brady, Elizabeth Patterson, Lyle Talbot, Isabel Jewell, Margaret Perry, Etienne Girardot, Xavier Cugat and his orchestra.

8. EVERY DAY'S A HOLIDAY. Paramount. 1938. *A. Edward Sutherland.*
Sp: Mae West. Cast: Edmund Lowe, Charles Butterworth, Charles Winninger,
Lloyd Nolan, Walter Catlett, Chester Conklin, Louis Armstrong.

9. MY LITTLE CHICKADEE. Universal. 1940. *Edward Cline.* Sp: Mae West
and W.C. Fields. Cast: W.C. Fields, Joseph Calleia, Dick Foran, Margaret
Hamilton, Donald Meek, Anne Nagel, Ruth Donnelly.

10. THE HEAT'S ON. Columbia. 1943. *Gregory Ratoff.* Sp: Fitzroy Davis,
George S. George, and Fred Schiller. Cast: Victor Moore, William Gaxton, Hazel
Scott, Lester Allen, Mary Roche, Almira Sessions, Xavier Cugat and his
orchestra.

11. MYRA BRECKENRIDGE. Twentieth Century-Fox. 1970. In color.
*Michael Sarne.* Sp: Michael Sarne and David Giles, b/o novel by Gore Vidal.
Cast: John Huston, Raquel Welch, Rex Reed, Roger Herren, Farrah Fawcett,
Calvin Lockhart, Andy Devine, John Carradine, George Furth.

# INDEX

## ABOUT THE AUTHOR

Michael Bavar is a playwright and stage director with a strong interest in film. He holds a doctorate degree in comparative literature from Columbia University and lives in New York City.

## ABOUT THE EDITOR

Ted Sennett is the author of *Warner Brothers Presents,* a tribute to the great Warners films of the Thirties and Forties, and of *Lunatics and Lovers,* on the long-vanished but well-remembered "screwball" comedies of the past. He is also the editor of *The Movie Buff's Book* and has written about films for magazines and newspapers. He lives in New Jersey with his wife and three children.